PENGUIN HANDBOOKS PH 51

Hardy Herbaceous Plants

LANNING ROPER

Lanning Roper, an American by birth, was educated in the United States, graduating from Harvard in 1933. He then taught at Buckley School in New York City, and travelled extensively during vacations, visiting gardens in various countries. In 1942 he was commissioned Ensign in the U.S. Navy. Duty brought him to England, where he spent his spare time studying British flora and landscape design.

After the war he returned to London to represent an American business firm, but resigned to become a student, first at Kew and later at the Royal Botanic Garden, Edinburgh. He visited many gardens in Britain and on the Continent. In 1951 he joined the staff of the Royal Horticultural Society as Assistant to the Editor, resigning in 1957 to take up free-lance journalism and garden design. Mr Roper contributes to the horticultural press in this country and America. He is the author of *The Gardens in the Royal Parks at Windsor* and *Successful Town Gardening*. The garden which he and his artist wife, Primrose Harley, have made in Kensington is well known.

The illustration on the cover is of *Paeonia mlokosewitschii*.

Eryngium

LANNING ROPER

HARDY
HERBACEOUS
PLANTS

Prepared in conjunction and collaboration with
The Royal Horticultural Society

PENGUIN BOOKS

Penguin Books Ltd, Harmondsworth, Middlesex
U.S.A. : Penguin Books Inc., 3300 Clipper Mill Road, Baltimore 11, Md
AUSTRALIA : Penguin Books Pty Ltd, 762 Whitehorse Road,
Mitcham, Victoria

First published 1960
Reprinted 1961

Copyright © Lanning Roper, 1960

Made and printed in Great Britain
by Jarrold and Sons Limited
Norwich

Contents

List of Plates

Propagation of Herbaceous Plants

Root Cuttings

Layering a Border Carnation

Seasonal Operations

Plants for Woodland Gardens

Outstanding Border Plants

Propagation of Delphiniums

Acknowledgements

This book has been written to help all those who grow hardy herbaceous plants in their gardens. It is designed primarily for the beginner, but there is much material that should prove useful to the more experienced as well. Plans of borders have been omitted as they are readily available in catalogues and other books on herbaceous plants.

I am indebted to Mr J. E. Downward, F.I.B.P., who has taken the majority of the photographs, to the Director, the Curator, and many members of the Wisley staff for their willing assistance in staging demonstrations and for their constructive criticism of practical matters in my text, to Mr Bertram Unné for the photograph used in Plate 17, to Colonial Williamsburg for permission to reproduce Plate 20, to the British Overhead Irrigation Co. Ltd for the photograph used in Plate 46, to Mr A. S. Mould for the photograph used for Plate 52 and taken in Mrs Margery Fish's garden at East Lambrook Manor, to the Shell Photographic Unit for Plates 96 to 103, to Mr N. K. Gould of the Wisley staff for Plate 107, to Messrs Allwood Bros. for Plates 80 to 82, to Messrs Sutton & Sons for Plate 140, to Mr R. Parrett for Plate 144, and to the late Mr W. A. Waarey for Plate 145. I have been assisted with kindness by many nurserymen and growers and by kind friends who have allowed their gardens and plants to be specially photographed in the interests of this publication. I am particularly grateful to Mr Patrick M. Synge for his wise counsel and enthusiastic help in the compilation of this book.

1. *Stachys lanata* spilling over a paved terrace in a country garden.

2. A fine example of a well-planned herbaceous border.

1 · The Nature of
Hardy Herbaceous Plants

Before we can consider the great range of hardy herbaceous plants
and the diversity of their uses in modern gardening we must
define what we mean by both the terms herbaceous and hardy.
By herbaceous plants we mean those plants of a non-woody
nature which grow each year from a persistent root-stock and
then die back to ground level in winter. By hardy plants we mean
those herbaceous plants which live for several or more seasons in
our gardens and do not die after flowering and producing seed as
is the habit of annuals and true biennials. Examples of hardy
herbaceous plants abound on every side, and include well-known
favourites of flower gardens such as oriental poppies, delphiniums, lupins, phloxes, and Michaelmas daisies, as well as the
primroses, celandines, and buttercups of country lanes. In the
vegetable garden asparagus and rhubarb are perfect examples of
hardy herbaceous plants, as are the chives, mint, tarragon, and
fennel in the herb border. Turning to fruits, the strawberry is a
charming and delicious example. To our lasting grief, at times
fury, herbaceous weeds are also hardy, as all who have had to
contend with bindweed, ground elder, sow thistle, and couch
grass have discovered.

Here at the outset we find difficulty. What of bergenias with
their persistent leathery leaves, the glaucous foliage of pinks, or
the woolly leaves of lamb's tongue (*Stachys lanata*) (Plate 1),
which are often persistent in a mild winter? Yet we claim all these
as herbaceous plants. Furthermore, a plant that dies to the ground
in a cold climate may fail to do so in a warm one.

Quite obviously in the scope of this short book the field of
hardy herbaceous plants must be narrowed to those plants which
are decorative, primarily because of their flowers, foliage, and
habit. The additional factor of fragrance is also worth consider-
ing, for this too plays a large part in the delight of our gardens.
So much of the charm of a cottage garden or border depends on

15

3. *Trillium grandiflorum* and primulas naturalized in a
   woodland garden.

the fragrance of phlox, spicy pinks, evening primroses, paeonies, and the like. The field of herbaceous plants is still too vast. We must rule out the majority of plants which are essentially suited to specialized forms of gardening, such as alpine and rock gardens, although there are many of these, like the lovely flaxes or dwarf erigerons which we arbitrarily retain as suitable for clumps along the front of an herbaceous border.

At the outset I want to make it plain that this book is not intended solely for the devotees of herbaceous borders (Plate 2). The gardener of today may well prefer to abandon this limiting form of gardening in favour of the mixed border containing shrubs, roses, herbaceous plants, and perhaps quantities of bulbs as well. This will extend the range of interest and may better conform to the size of his property, the depths of his pocket, and the labour available. Then there is the wild or woodland garden, where primulas, Solomon's seals, trilliums (Plate 3), blue poppies (*Meconopsis*), foxgloves, and scores of other shade-loving plants are seen to advantage, and the bog garden (Plates 4, 5) where still other herbaceous plants such as moisture-loving irises, rheums, astilbes, kingcups, and ferns are completely happy. There are small properties, whether country, suburban, or town, where all

4. Feathery astilbes and Japanese irises growing in a moist border.

5. A bog garden with giant gunneras, rodgersias in foreground, and *Peltiphyllum peltatum* in left centre.

6. Regale lilies, roses, and herbaceous plants in a typical cottage garden.

manner of plants – annuals, biennials, and herbaceous – grow in harmony with roses, shrubs, and climbers to create delightful gardens, full of individuality and charm. We have only to look at the cottage garden (Plate 6) overflowing with pinks, wallflowers, roses, madonna lilies, lilacs, snapdragons, valerian, and honeysuckle to see the possibilities. Today many larger gardens are being adapted along similar lines, with admirable results.

Besides their decorative use in gardens, herbaceous plants are a valuable source of cut flowers. Each year there is an increasing demand for them as a result of the popular interest in flower arrangement on the part of women and men alike. This enthusiasm has stimulated not only a demand for larger quantities but also for unusual varieties. Today beds and borders for cutting often supplant the old type of exhibition herbaceous border, and in larger gardens supplement them. Rows or blocks of pyrethrums, scabious (Plate 7), doronicums, delphiniums, alstroemerias, and varieties of the large white daisy, *Chrysanthemum maximum* (Plate 8), are grown for the house, and plants like yarrow (*Achillea*), sea lavender, thrift, honesty, and larkspur are cut and dried for winter bouquets. This book also deals with this aspect of

7. *Scabiosa caucasica*, excellent for cutting.

8. *Chrysanthemum maximum* 'Horace Read', a long-lasting white daisy.

herbaceous flowers, but of course does not consider the production of cut flowers for market, as this is a specialized problem.

In dealing with hardy herbaceous plants, especially in beds and borders, certain plants belonging to different categories inevitably creep into the scheme, and these by their usefulness and suitability deserve a recognized place. As a result, these same plants may also be discussed in other volumes in this series of gardening books, particularly those dealing with flowering shrubs, bulbs, hardy annuals, and biennials. A perfect example is lavender, beloved for its low, spreading masses of silvery foliage and spikes of spicy mauve and purple flowers (Plate 9). It is certainly a shrub by definition, but so happy is it in association with herbaceous plants that to my mind it is a delightful addition to borders, just as it is to rose gardens. So too yuccas, though most certainly not herbaceous by definition, have an important place in borders and in other planting schemes predominantly herbaceous. Then there is the question as to where biennials belong, as the devotees of herbaceous borders and the lovers of hardy annuals can both stake a legitimate claim. To my mind, Canterbury bells, sweet williams, and foxgloves are as much at home in herbaceous gardens as in the display reserved for annuals, more so in fact because of their habit and time of flowering. Therefore I have included the more outstanding ones, though they can be considered perennial only on certain soils and in certain localities.

Dahlias and chrysanthemums are enjoying unprecedented popularity today. Dahlias are certainly not hardy, nor are many types of chrysanthemums, but by the nature of their propagation, cultivation, and use they must obviously both be included in this book. Lastly we come to that large group of hardy plants including bulbs, corms, and tubers. Again my treatment is an arbitrary one, usefulness, suitability, time of flowering, and hardiness being the criteria for inclusion. Madonna, regale, and tiger lilies are certainly suitable for herbaceous borders and mixed plantings. The stately summer-flowering hyacinth *Galtonia candicans* with its white bells, the delightful magenta *Gladiolus byzantinus*, hardy montbretias, and crinums are highly effective in the herbaceous border, and therefore find a place in this book as well as in a similar one which will be devoted to bulbs.

9. Beds of irises and lavender with large-leaved bergenias in foreground.

I make no apologies for the latitude in my terms of reference, because I think that it is in keeping with the economic and social demands of modern gardening and because I have a shrewd suspicion that it most probably coincides with gardening traditions of the past – Greek, Roman, Medieval, and European. The purist herbaceous border is in all probability of comparative recent development, for its first great exponents were William Robinson and Miss Gertrude Jekyll some fifty years ago. Before that there are indications of the segregation of herbaceous plants in the journals and literary works of eighteenth- and even seventeenth-century writers. But these are brief, and it is often easy to read into them whatever one wishes, although in Philip Miller's *Dictionary of Gardening* (1724) there is an undeniable reference to what was the forerunner of the herbaceous border. Furthermore, in monastery gardens and later in physic and botanic gardens there were undoubtedly collections of hardy herbaceous plants, but these were not being raised primarily for decorative effect.

I think it must be admitted that the herbaceous border purely for effect is of British origin and that it stems primarily from William Robinson and Miss Jekyll. It was the product of an age when labour was cheap, money was plentiful, and interest in horticulture was running on the crest of the tide. Furthermore, it developed in the country where conditions were ideal for the cultivation of herbaceous plants as the result of the equitable climate, free from extremes of hot and cold, and of the rainfall, adequate and well distributed throughout the year. It is not without reason, then, that these spectacular displays are not so successfully duplicated in any other country and remain a feature peculiar to British gardening to be admired by tourists in increasing numbers. Heat and drought are both arch enemies of herbaceous borders and for that matter of lawns, for what is grass but a hardy herbaceous plant.

General Requirements for Successful Cultivation

There are herbaceous plants for almost every conceivable position, for they are adapted to the variations of soil, temperature, and rainfall found in the different localities of the country. Plants with grey foliage, like artemisias, and blue and grey thistles, such as echinops and eryngiums, will grow on almost any soil, even if dry and poor, as long as they have sunshine and sufficient depth of root run. Others, like phloxes, columbines, and bleeding hearts, require rich soil and ample moisture until they have flowered, while Japanese irises, king cups, and lysichitons grow in bog conditions or even with their feet in running water. The lovely wand flower (*Dierama pulcherrimum*) and meconopsis like an acid soil; pinks and garden irises thrive on chalk. Alstroemerias (Plate 10), poppies, and gaillardias like sunshine and light soils; lilies of the valley, hellebores, and trilliums demand semi-shade, while hostas and day lilies (hemerocallis) are obligingly happy in shade or sun as long as they have enough moisture at the roots. Thus we see the diversity of the requirements of herbaceous plants.

Generally speaking, there are two factors which are essentials for successful cultivation – air and light. Those who have tried to grow plants in a dank back garden where these requisites are

10. *Alstroemeria* Ligtu Hybrids, growing in full sun on warm light soil.

lacking will know only too well what I mean. Furthermore, all herbaceous plants require good drainage and will not tolerate sodden sour soil no matter how moisture-loving they may be. Heavy clay soils imperfectly drained are the worst offenders, as air must be present in the soil between the particles. It is this lack of air in heavy soils, where there are very fine particles which become completely suspended in water, that causes plants to deteriorate and decay. Air must be free to circulate around the growth above ground as well. That is why it is a mistake to bank perennials thickly next to a wall without room for the circulation of air behind them.

In choosing a site, air and good drainage must be first considerations. If the last is not satisfactory, then in the preparation of the site before planting special measures must be taken. If this cannot be accomplished by the improvement of the soil itself, then more drastic corrective measures must be undertaken by a system of underground drains, sump holes filled with coarse rubble, stones, or gravel, or even by the digging of an open ditch. The last, of course, is possible in a woodland garden but not in the midst of an herbaceous border (Plate 11).

Herbaceous plants, particularly tall and fragile ones, need protection from wind. It snaps the heavy spikes of delphiniums, knocks lupins down like ninepins, and breaks off the giant stalks of bocconias, hollyhocks, heliopsis, and monkshoods (aconitums), so proud before the storm. A wall would seem to be the answer, but this is not always so, as there are unaccountable eddies, whirlwinds, and down-draughts which wreck havoc. Herbaceous plants require not only protection from prevailing blasts but adequate support as well because of the weight of the flower heads, especially when deluged with rain. We always couple the words warm and sheltered with a wall with a southerly aspect, but there is no guarantee that a border planted in its lee will be free from wind and hence not require staking. On this subject much will be said later.

Ample food and water are the next essentials, as these are inextricably linked with good cultivation. Herbaceous plants, with their large masses of foliage and flowers, require both in considerable quantity if they are to flourish. These two requirements must be taken into consideration when the ground is being prepared to assure long-term nourishment and adequate moisture-retention properties to enable strong growth. Subsequent watering and feeding will also be required to meet the individual needs of particular varieties. A high standard of cultivation to maintain a good soil tilth is essential to prevent excessive evaporation of moisture. Mulches applied before evaporation has become excessive will promote the same end.

Weeds must be removed assiduously, as they compete with the plants for food, moisture, air, and light. Never forget that weeds are essentially the same as the plants you are so lovingly cultivating and that plants are only weeds because they are growing in the wrong place. Weeds must not be allowed to establish and grow into the roots of herbaceous plants, or it may become necessary to destroy the clumps. For this reason make sure that new plants from nurseries are perfectly clean, as a bit of

11. A ditch which has been developed into a small stream for moisture-loving plants. Note bold leaves of *Lysichitum americanum* with candelabra primulas.

convolvulus or ground elder lurking in a paeony or clump of phlox can infect a whole section of a border. But the most compelling of all arguments against weeds is the fact that they are unsightly.

Lastly, if borders are to be healthy they must be free of pests and diseases. Field mice, slugs, green fly, mildew, and dozens of other plagues, designed like weeds to mar the gardener's paradise, cause rapid and costly devastation. Vigilance and foresight are both required. Snails or slugs alone, for example, can do untold havoc, reducing the hostas to a system of lacework and completely wiping out the new shoots of delphiniums. (For control see p. 135.)

The novice should learn as much as he can about the physical characteristics of herbaceous plants, for these often explain their requirements and even their idiosyncrasies in connexion with methods of propagation, their longevity, need for lifting, dividing, or even their intolerance of interference, as the case may be. In other words, familiarity with the root system and habits of a plant will enable the good gardener to satisfy its wants, even if it is only to be left undisturbed for years, as is the case with paeonies with large, tough, fleshy roots and *Campanula lactiflora*. Part of the challenge for the beginner is the mastery of enough knowledge to enable him to avoid the more obvious mistakes, such as throwing away the two plants listed above when they fail to settle down in the first year or even to give a good account of themselves in the second. This is one of the purposes of this book, just as I hope that it will enable you to cut back or dead-head the phlox, pyrethrums, or delphiniums in such a way as to ensure a second flush of flowers.

Labour Requirements of Herbaceous Plants

As in all forms of gardening, herbaceous plants make special demands on labour, many of which have already been hinted at. The initial preparation of the ground must be as thorough as possible. Planting must be painstaking and exacting, with subsequent cultivation, feeding, and watering carried out with thoroughness and intelligence to obtain good results. All this requires labour, but the important thing is to learn to use it properly

12. Herbaceous plants cleverly used in an informal country garden made on different levels. Note good staking of larger plants.

and efficiently and at the right times. Then there is the matter of staking which plays such a vital role in the appearance of a border (Plate 12). True, healthy plants are strong and require less support than plants that are weak and drawn for lack of light, but even so, many herbaceous plants are so tall and of such a habit that they cannot stand up to winds and the weight of rain on their own. Even the finest borders if improperly staked will not be effective after the first bout with the elements, and once the damage has been done it can never be repaired. There are, of course, many plants that require no staking, and these I will try to single out.

Dead-heading or housemaiding the border is time-consuming, but it is amply repaid, not only by the neat appearance but also by the increase in the vigour and prolonged flowering of the plants. Come the autumn, there is the task of clearing up, restoring order where plants have encroached upon each other, the rearrangement

27

of groupings, and dozens of other jobs as well. In other words the successful cultivation of herbaceous plants requires hard work, especially if they are planted in a border devoted exclusively to them. The garden owner who employs no labour and has very little spare time should not undertake an herbaceous border lightly. He had better resort to a mixed border of shrubs and herbaceous plants or to a wild garden if opportunity permits, but even with these there are demands in plenty. The important thing is to be realistic. I have tried to convey to the beginner a fair picture of some of the more urgent problems that will beset him, besides the obvious ones of planting and reaping the harvest.

Tools and Supplies for the Herbaceous Garden

The tools required are not very different from those needed for other forms of gardening. Two tools are essential, a narrow, sharp spade with a long blade and a fork. A steel rake and either a Dutch hoe or a three- or five-pronged cultivator are invaluable for working among plants to maintain a good tilth and to scratch up weeds. Besides these a hand fork, a trowel, secateurs, a sharp knife, a line with two stakes for trenching and edging, a wheel barrow, and a trug basket will all be needed. Lastly there should, if possible, and this implies a place for storage, be an adequate supply of well-rotted manure, compost, leaf mould, coarse sand, bone meal, lime, ground chalk, and various fertilizers and insecticides as necessary. A watering-can with a fine rose will have multiple uses, and other watering apparatus may be required. Bamboo canes, pea brush, raffia, and bast will be needed for support, and very probably heavier stakes as well. This list sounds formidable, but whether you start with them all or not, they are the things that will be needed in time. Anyway, most of them will be in the garden shed already if there are other gardening operations under way. If I were going to give myself a present I should include a small strong fork and spade such as a twelve-year-old child would use, as they are invaluable for lifting plants, dividing small tenacious clumps with matted roots, working in surface dressings among the plants, and pricking over the surface to ensure a good tilth.

2 · Planning the Herbaceous Garden

I have deliberately omitted the word border from the title of this chapter, as so much that I will say applies to the mixed border, the informal cottage garden, and even to formal gardens where herbaceous flowers are grown in rectangular beds as part of a larger scheme. The planning phase is one of the most important, for it is at this stage, as in a military engagement, that the essential pattern of subsequent operations is laid down. Few gardeners are fortunate enough to be able to choose the site of the garden so that the climate, soil, and topography are in accordance with their needs. Rather it is the house which is generally selected for its charm, convenience, accessibility, and setting, the garden coming as a secondary consideration.

It is usually easier and certainly less expensive to adapt the garden to the site rather than the site to a garden which has been preconceived. As a matter of fact, both will go hand in hand, for much as one may want a double border there may only be room for a single one. In selecting the site, satisfactory conditions for the successful cultivation of plants must be obtainable, but it is equally important to locate the border or beds so that they are effective and can be enjoyed. Today, with the marked tendency to integrate the house with the garden, an attempt should be made to allow the border to be enjoyed from the principal rooms of the house or from the veranda or terrace which has proved the focal point of outdoor living (Plate 13). Sometimes this may not be in conjunction with the house but with a garden house or paved area under a spreading tree, from which the border may be enjoyed (Plates 14, 15). Less and less are large borders at a distance from the house practical or desirable, although borders in the kitchen garden can be delightful (Plate 16).

One-sided borders are probably the most common, and certainly easier to design than those seen from two sides or from all four, as is the case with beds set in lawns or paved terraces. The one-sided border usually has a wall or hedge or trellis as a

13. A mixed border backed by a yew hedge in a pool garden.

14. A double border flanking a grass path in mid-summer.

15. A low border along a terrace balustrade.

16. Loose herbaceous borders backed by apple trees in a kitchen garden.

31

background and is seen either from the front, as across an open lawn, or close at hand as one walks down a path or terrace (Plate 13). Obviously each will require different treatment, as one will be seen in its entirety, the other at an angle and at close range. The one-sided border may either be rectangular in plan, with a straight edge along the front, or it may be gently curving in plan or, as is so often the case, be laid out in sinuous natural curves, harmonious with shrubberies and the contours of the land. In the one-sided border the general rule is to plant the taller subjects towards the back and to bring the lower plants well forward, although often higher groupings towards the front break the monotony and add an element of mystery, as in this way the length of the border can no longer be seen at a sweeping glance.

The two-sided border creates a very different problem, as it no longer is a set piece against a wall or hedge but exists in space so that it can be seen and enjoyed from both sides. Often such a border is made within a lawn or along the edge of a path or terrace with a lawn or another path beyond. Here the tendency is to group the taller plants to the centre so that there are lower-spreading perennials along both fronts. This type of border poses more problems than the one-sided border, as the gardener must think of the subject from every angle.

So far our discussion has been limited to single borders, but there are the double borders as well which flank a broad path or a grass vista. The two sets of herbaceous borders in The Royal Horticultural Society's Gardens at Wisley are excellent examples, though on a scale few private gardeners will care to emulate. The old borders on the way to the restaurant flank a wide grass path, while the new even deeper mixed shrub and herbaceous borders backed by hornbeam on the gentle slope leading to Battleston Hill frame a broad grass vista. This is also the case at Newby Hall in Yorkshire, where wide borders backed by yew frame a lovely view to the river (Plate 17). Double borders on a much smaller scale flank the front path to many a cottage or villa door or the central axis of a garden. In designing borders on any scale the relation of masses and forms, as well as of colour groupings, must be kept in mind. Complete symmetry in double borders can become formal and monotonous.

17. Large-scale borders flanking a grassy vista from the house to the river.

Selection of the Site

A cardinal factor in siting the border will be its proper orientation. Although local conditions may impose exceptional limitations, generally a border should run east and west so that the border will face south or in a southerly sector, such as south-east or south-west, the latter being preferable. Borders facing due east or north are not desirable, although if there is no other option because of the lie of the land, satisfactory borders are still possible, but they must be specially planted with semi-shade-loving plants (see Appendix L). Actually these lend themselves better to a mixed border than to a strictly herbaceous one. In cities and towns properties with such limitations are not uncommon, and a border should not be ruled out. Where freedom of choice is allowed, it would be madness to make a wrong choice. Lastly, it should be remembered that borders in the open are very different from those against the high walls of buildings, for light and air help to compensate for lack of sunshine. The importance of these two cannot be over emphasized as they are essential to healthy strong growth and do much to prevent both diseases and pests. How right is the old maxim that an ounce of prevention is worth a pound of cure. Air, light, and good drainage are a large part of the ounce.

I have heard more than one gardener rule out a site for a border because it was sloping. This is invalid, as delightful and original effects can be achieved on gently sloping ground and there are no practical problems if the ground is properly graded when dug. Of course, herbaceous plants by their nature will help to prevent soil erosion during torrential rains.

Perennials do not like the shade of overhanging trees. If possible, direct shade should be avoided, but we all know the charm of an old apple tree or a flowering cherry growing in a border, and there are obliging plants like epimediums, hostas, campanulas, lilies of the valley, and sweet rocket which are happy in its shade. Sun-loving plants if grown in the shade of trees or even of a wall will tend to thin, attenuated growth, often growing out at an angle towards the light rather than up straight. This increases the problems of staking and of course destroys the natural habit of the plants. Flowers will be few in numbers and colours may be pale. It must be remembered that brilliant colours of certain plants, particularly bright orange and scarlet phloxes, are badly bleached by too brilliant sun, and partial shade is preferable. This challenge to get the best from every plant is part of the fun when planning herbaceous plantings.

Backgrounds

Just as the proper background is important for pictures or flower arrangements, so it is for the herbaceous border. Backgrounds fall into three groups – walls, hedges, and trellises and fences, which must be considered as one. The first includes the walls of buildings, including houses, stables, and outbuildings, as well as terrace walls and garden walls (Plate 18). To this matter of backgrounds we must apply two criteria, the one practical, the other aesthetic. As usual, to arrive at a decision both must be balanced. Walls offer a solid background, and though an excellent wind shield, they do not eliminate the staking of the border, as there are curious draughts and eddies produced by a wall which may cause havoc. A south wall, of course, holds the heat, offering the best shelter for tender plants and making for an early border.

18. Wide borders backed by shrubbery with a walled border at the far end. Note the verbascums in narrow beds in the grass.

By the same token, in hot, dry localities plants will be subjected to even severer heat and drought, especially on light soils, and many may flag if not watered. Walls are, of course, expensive to build, but have the advantage of not requiring upkeep, and unlike hedges they have no roots to encroach on the border and to impoverish the soil. Aesthetically walls are charming, as the warm red or pink of old brick is flattering to flowers and foliage alike. Even more attractive is the cool grey of stone, which enhances almost any shade of flower, and the yellowish cast of the local stones in parts of Somerset and Gloucestershire is a wonderful warm background. Modern red brick is often harsh, and strong yellows may be ugly against it. Terrace walls, if of sufficient height, are a charming background, and there is the added pleasure of looking down on the flowers from above.

Hedges, while providing beautiful backgrounds, pose problems. Aesthetically there is no more attractive foil for flowers than the close-textured green mass of a well-grown yew hedge (Plate 13). Yew is supposedly slow-growing, but with 18- to 24-inch plants a good hedge should be tall enough to make a suitable background

35

in eight to ten years. If larger plants are set out, at considerably more expense, the process is accelerated. Everyone agrees that yew makes a superb background. Yet there are difficulties. Like other hedges, it must be clipped once a year, preferably in mid-summer or very early autumn. It is not immune to pests, and it is hungry and thirsty as well, robbing the border of nutrients which must be put back. Lastly, although yew is tolerant of shade, if we plant too close to it the lower part will gradually die back.

As yew has its drawbacks, let us explore other possibilities. Holly hedges are magnificent, but they are even more expensive to plant, slow-growing, and I for one have had too many painful altercations with dead holly leaves in shrubberies to relish them in a border. Beech and hornbeam are attractive, but of course deciduous and very vigorous with encroaching roots (Plate 19). They are far cheaper to plant than yew and faster growing. The feathery green of *Cupressus macrocarpa* and *Chamaecyparis lawsoniana* are attractive and they both develop rapidly into a good hedge, but they tend to grow thin at the bottom, and except on light soils and in relatively mild areas the former is subject to frost damage in severe winters. Both these, though less expensive than yew, are costly, and of course require annual clipping. Quickest growing of all evergreen hedges is the hybrid *C. leylandii*. *Lonicera nitida* is fast-growing, fine textured, inexpensive, and easy, as cuttings strike freely. In seaside areas where the weather is mild tamarisk and pittosporum are possible, and *Escallonia macrantha* is ideal, with its good foliage and rosy-crimson flowers. Privet hedges are evergreen, foolproof, cheap, and quick-growing, all desirable characteristics, but are too voracious and tend to grow too leggy to make the ideal hedge. *Berberis stenophylla* is a lovely dark-green hedge, but invasive. Mixed tapestry hedges are effective but slow and require careful trimming, as the growing seasons for the components are apt to vary.

I have dealt with hedges in some detail. As they must frame the border and last its life, they are vitally important. Mistakes with herbaceous plants are in most cases easily rectified. Not so hedges. A few basic rules. Don't economize on hedging material. It is better to plant a cheaper kind than yew, macrocarpa, or holly

19. Large clumps of white crambe (*C. cordifolia*) giving height and form to a large border.

than to skimp on numbers or to plant a single row when a double staggered row is required. Try to curb your impatience if possible, as smaller, cheaper stock makes eventually the thickest hedge. Nurserymen will give expert advice on numbers required and the pattern of planting, as well as estimates of cost. Feed your hedge as well as your flowers, particularly yew. Prune, even at the expense of top growth, to thicken the bottom while plants are young. Cut back the roots as necessary if they encroach too deeply among the plants. Lastly, be sure to leave at least 2 to 3 feet between the wall or hedge and the back range of herbaceous plants. This will provide air and access.

Now a few comments on arbours and fences (Plate 20) are in order. There are many types of both. When planted with rambler roses, climbers, vines, and ivies, trellises are attractive and useful as boundaries where properties are small. They occupy little space, are inexpensive, and offer great variety of design and texture. Fences are particularly suited to small-scale borders. All posts for insertion in the ground should be of durable wood like larch or chestnut which have been boiled or treated with creosote or tar.

20. A white picket fence used as a low background with box hedges as edging.

Scale of the Border

The width of a border depends on various factors, particularly on the height of the background and its length. The higher the wall and the greater its length, the wider the border should be for effectiveness. It is impossible to lay down hard-and-fast rules, but a narrow border at the base of a protected wall is far better devoted to an interesting collection of unusual plants combining herbaceous plants with shrubs, climbers, and bulbous plants, such as fuchsias, carpenterias, crinums, agapanthus, nerines, shrubby salvias, and a host of others dictated by personal preferences. These will give a much better effect than a long, narrow bed of herbaceous plants, which could never provide sufficient display for a protracted period. An herbaceous border narrower than 5 feet, even if devoted to low-growing plants, is seldom effective. Borders should be at least 7 to 10 feet in width, not including the space eventually to be occupied by a hedge, and may be increased to 15 or 18 feet as long as sufficient width is left at the rear for access. A path of paving-stones is a great asset, as it makes it possible to penetrate the border at the back even when sodden with rain. If borders are too wide the problem of upkeep becomes enormous and the number of plants required is staggering. There is no reason, however, for limiting the width as long as the length is in proportion. Most of us are fortunately not concerned with borders of vast dimensions.

Scale of Planting

There have been various rules laid down for the relative width of a border and the height of the plants. Some advocate that the height of plants should not exceed half the width of the border. This means that in the 10-feet border the tallest groups should not exceed 5 feet, while in a 15-foot border the tallest groups would average between 7 and 8 feet. Others increase the height of the plantings by a quarter to a third. I myself think that much must depend on the height of the background and the length of the border. The plants in a very long border should probably be higher than in a short one, while a border against a high wall should be taller than one against a low terrace wall, both for practical and aesthetic reasons. I personally advocate variation in heights with, say, a taller group or two of delphiniums near the end to give it weight or here and there a huge cloud of white gypsophila, crambe (Plate 19), or giant thistles to form a variation in the otherwise carefully graded heights. Here the genius of the gardener comes into play and each must evolve his own type of border. Some will have the plants evenly graduated down from back to front to give a sloping bank of colour. Others will have undulating high masses brought forward, with here and there lower ones carried back. Others will alternate the height of the plants at the back, so that masses can be seen silhouetted against the background of wall or yew. These techniques develop with experience, but it is better for the novice to be guided by the first rule of thumb mentioned above.

Closely allied with the matter of height and the actual dimensions of the border is the problem of the size of the individual groups. Obviously the smaller border will have clumps proportionately reduced. Midget borders, or miniature borders, so-called, may have only three plants to a group, while a border 8 to 10 feet wide may have five, seven, or even ten. In a 15- to 20-foot border groups of a dozen, eighteen, or even twenty-four may be effectively employed. There is no rule. Nor is there a fixed code about uniformity of size of the groups. In many borders professionally designed all groups are roughly uniform in size. Personally, I prefer to vary the size and shape of the group according to the subject. If a plant is large, bold, and dynamic, one or three may be sufficient to provide the necessary spikiness, solidity, or even a lacy cloud of bloom, while it may take a dozen or more to achieve an effect with a subtle, unobtrusive, but delightful plant. The lovely starry-flowered astrantias, with their delicate green and rose tones, are a case in point.

The area that a single plant occupies, the time of its flowering, and its habit afterwards are all factors of paramount importance. For example, the delightful blue *Geranium grandiflorum*, which is lovely in the front rank of a border with its large mauve-purple flowers in June and lasting on into July, has attractive and persistent foliage which will not leave a gap in the border. Therefore a good clump is desirable, though not too large a one, as its blooming season finishes early. Bleeding hearts, one of the most graceful of border plants, is seen to best advantage when three or five plants are widely spaced to show off the graceful arching racemes of pendulous pink-and-white flowers. After flowering in June the foliage dies down, often completely. If a very large clump were to be used, it would be difficult to have surrounding plants to cover the area. It is considerations such as these which the experienced gardener will know how to meet.

In summary it is important, especially for the timid beginner, to decide on the scheme which he wishes to follow, remembering that it will be easier to lay out the plan with roughly even groups. Experimentation in the sizes and shapes of groups will come with experience and confidence. But the more daring novice should have a try at both in his first border and may not regret it.

Frontal Treatment of the Border

The outer edge of any border poses certain problems. If the front is a straight one there are various possibilities of treatment. Much depends on whether the border is bounded by a path, a terrace of paving, gravel, or pebble or by mown lawn. A paved front means that the border can spill out loosely, encroaching as is the habit of the different plants. Thus we achieve a lovely loose edge, with each variety of plant growing in its natural character (Plate 21). Where there is a grass verge all too often clumps are placed far back from the edge so that when fully developed they will not encroach and make mowing difficult or kill the grass where they spill over it, or if planted too close to the grass they are staked and restrained. Here is a matter for individual taste, but I prefer a loose, free edge in keeping with the exuberance of perennials.

Where a straight border adjoins turf a single course of paving-stones or a brick edge a foot or 18 inches in width is a good solution (Plate 22). It will save labour, and if the stones are very closely set, or even pointed so that weeds cannot grow in the joints, this is a still further benefit. If stone slabs prove too expensive, as they well may, and no supply of old ones already exists as a stockpile, concrete slabs can be treated with manure water to colour and age them. In any case I heartily approve of this use of

21. Geraniums, sun roses, and poppies spilling out over a paved path.

22. A row of flagstones along the front edge of a border allows a loose edge. Grass will be allowed to grow to edge of paving.

stones, although many gardeners are opposed to it, some saying that it makes the front of the border badly drained and encourages slugs to collect and breed under cover of the plants, though this contingency can be coped with by improving drainage of the soil. This form of paved edging is, of course, less suitable to curving borders.

When planning the front edge there is a choice of having clumps of low-growing perennials or of here and there breaking the flatness with taller mounds. Another school of thought advocates a continuous edging with nepeta, dwarf box, or a lavender hedge. The solution will be dictated by the overall scheme and by labour and practicability. Certainly box edgings (Plate 20), lovely as they are, are fast disappearing, especially from the kitchen garden.

3 · Preparation of the Plan –
Colour versus Form

The important thing about any plan is that it is to scale. Correct measurements of the actual border and an indication of shady patches on the plan are also vital factors. Large sheets of squared paper are admirable for the purpose, and a convenient scale can be evolved. An inch to a foot for a small border or an inch to a yard is probably most practical, although it may not be possible to indicate the exact placing of each plant and its name as well. For the experienced gardener the former is not essential, as a number will indicate the total number of plants in a group. For the beginner it is advantageous to indicate the position of each plant, as it will make him concentrate on the habit of the plant and its spread in addition to its height, foliage characteristics, and colour.

Groups should be compact with extra space between them so that the form of the border will be improved. Otherwise plants tend to grow together, forming indeterminate masses. The actual density of planting is controversial. Much depends on the size of one's purse and one's patience. If a very presentable border is required the first season, planting will have to be much thicker, especially if the border is planted in spring instead of autumn, the relative merits of which are discussed on p. 66. Where money is a consideration, with quickly established plants like monardas, Michaelmas daisies, achilleas, anchusas, and the like, there is no advantage in planting close. These will have to be divided and replanted as the result of overcrowding in a relatively few years. Other plants, like paeonies and dictamnus (Plate 23), which are slow to settle down and hate disturbance, should be planted in their proper positions, even though there seems a lot of waste space at first. Allow as much as 2 to 4 feet between vigorous paeonies. Their ultimate size is considerable and their beauty is dependent on full development. Delphiniums and lupins should be planted in clumps of three, five, seven or twelve, depending on

23. *Dictamnus albus*, a fine border plant which establishes slowly and resents disturbance.

the size and vigour of the varieties and the scale of the border. A density of three or five plants to the square yard is reasonable for many plants, and this may be increased to seven or nine for smaller ones such as linums, heucheras, and violas, remembering of course to allow double the space around the outer members of the group and those of the next group. To make this last point clear, smaller plants should be planted with 8 or 9 inches between them, larger plants with 12 or even 15 inches. Between groups there should be 16 inches and 24 to 30 inches respectively.

Plants are best in groups containing odd numbers. In other words, groups of 3, 5, and 7 are easier to space than 2, 4, 6,

24. *Echinops ritro*, commonly known as the globe thistle.

and 8. Above these figures it really doesn't matter so much, and in groups of 18 or 24 not at all. Some nurseries make special rates for groups of 3 and 5 instead of for dozens and half-dozens, showing their realization of the soundness of this principle and also revealing the prevalence today of small gardens where buying is in small numbers. Here another cautionary word on expense is in order. The costs of carriage and packing have advanced so much that it is wise to order plants in bulk when possible, as the cost of carriage for a few is almost as much as for double or triple that quantity. For this reason a multiplication of small orders from a series of different nurseries is an expensive form of amusement, especially if shillings count.

25. *Iris ochroleuca*, a bold border plant requiring good damp soil.

On the plan distribution of heights will be dictated by the nature of the border and by personal preferences. It is vital to remember the scale of the border as mentioned above and not to be carried away by catalogue descriptions. Avoid too many plants that are leafy and rank with flowers of not great character. Borders containing a preponderance of nondescript herbaceous plants like galega, echinops (Plate 24), lactuca, lysimachia, and eupatorium lack form and charm. Include plants of different habits, spikey ones like *Iris ochroleuca* (Plate 25), monkshoods, delphiniums, hollyhocks, lupins, and eremurus with massive flowering clumps of phlox, *Achillea* 'Gold Plate', sweet williams, and Michaelmas daisies; bold flowers with dynamic form and

26. The bold flowers of day lilies contrast happily with the spiky heads of lupins and galegas.

colour like oriental poppies, regale lilies, paeonies, and hemerocallis; with other plants which are feathery and light which will soften bold clumps and contrast with the distinct habits of plants mentioned above (Plate 26). To this last group belong *Gypsophila paniculata*, *Limonium latifolium*, thalictrums (Plate 27), London pride, and heucheras. Then there are the host of daisy-like flowers, all of which are poised to catch the light, including rose and crimson pyrethrums, white shasta daisies, yellow anthemis, mauve and blue erigerons, Korean chrysanthemums, heleniums, heliopsis, the enormous range of the aster family, etc.

27. The feathery heads and delicate leaves of *Thalictrum aquilegiifolium*.

Foliage and the Border

The foliage of a plant and its habit must always be considered. Grey- and silver-leaved plants are invaluable in themselves and useful in blending groupings of different colours: *Stachys lanata*, artemisias in variety, *Lychnis coronaria*, giant cardoons, thistles, glaucous-leaved hostas, *Veronica incana*, pinks in variety, woolly thyme, and even the tender *Senecio maritima*, *Centaurea gymnocarpa*, and the not too reliable *Verbascum bombyciferum* or *broussa* as it is also called (Plate 28). The last is a superb border plant, with its large silvery woolly leaves, but it is definitely biennial, and not easy on cold, heavy soil.

In choosing a plant remember that much depends on its habit. Avoid too many tall plants that will require staking, or if you use them intersperse them among groups that will help give support. Plants that tend to lose their lower leaves or turn yellow for several feet from the ground, such as hollyhocks and aconitums, should be concealed at the base by other plants. Plants with persisting foliage of distinction and a fine overall appearance can be featured. A tall-growing *Bocconia cordata* with its large heart-shaped leaves backed with silver is such a plant, and so is the smaller *Dictamnus albus* and the decorative hairy-leaved *Alchemilla mollis*. This last seeds very freely and may become a weed in certain gardens, but I value it highly for its beautiful leaves and cluster of small acid yellow flowers. Bergenias, hostas, rodgersias, and rheums are other fine foliage plants (Plates 29–31).

Colour Display

One of the great arts in planning an herbaceous border is to achieve the maximum in colour, which most gardeners value far more highly than form and texture, which we have just discussed. Borders can be designed for seasonal effect, such as early summer, mid-summer, and autumn. Spring borders entirely of perennials are not advised, as the choice is limited, the season of most of them is short, and the remainder of the year the border is colourless, and some of the best plants, like *Mertensia virginica* and *Fritillaria imperialis*, disappear completely, leaving awkward gaps. These spring perennials are far better suited to the mixed border,

28. Trumpet lilies and *Verbascum bombyciferum* contrast boldly with the silvery filigree of artemisias and the woolly leaves of *Stachys lanata*.

29. The rounded leathery leaves of bergenias with a clump of epimedium at upper right.

51

30. The graceful flower heads and undulate leaves of *Hosta elata*.

31. The bold palmate leaves of rodgersias are an excellent foil to the narrow leaves of day lilies.

where spring flowering shrubs and bulbs make a spectacular display, or to the wild garden, where semi-shaded conditions are perfect for the good cultivation of many of them. Summer and autumn borders and large beds devoted to a single genus like asters or paeonies are very spectacular, but today they are rarely seen except in large gardens. Most owners of small properties want a continuous display for as long a period as possible, and the above formulae are not practical. This means that in planning the border great thought must be given to a succession of flowers from June until frost, not only to ensure their inclusion but also the blending of their multiple colours.

Again there are many theories. One gardener prefers bold groups of colour here and there to a general overall distribution. For example, a mass of flaming phlox may be the particular feature in one section of the border, bronze heleniums in another, and azure blue *Salvia patens* with silvery *Artemisia* 'Silver Queen' in a third. Another gardener would have small clumps of phlox repeated here and there, the colours being chosen to blend, with the heleniums and salvias used in a similar way. There is no doubt that spectacular effects can be achieved by large patches of a single variety, but repetition and blending of colours makes for a unity of composition and conforms to the older conception of a border.

Much depends on the scale of the border. If it is small there will probably be little room for repeats, save of particular favourites. Plans can be made for each month and the colours of the different groups indicated with crayon, pastel, or water-colour. This will show the distribution of colour and the juxtapositions throughout as the seasons progress. Less complicated are plans where colours themselves are not indicated but shading or cross hatching shows areas providing colour at a given month or season. Such plans are a considerable task, but can yield surprisingly good results.

The arrangement of colours within the border may have a definite pattern. I have seen most successful borders carried out entirely with pastel colours – pale pinks, blues, mauves, lavenders, and soft yellows with masses of whites and off-whites, including the subtle milky white of *Campanula lactiflora* and its varieties (Plate 32), the curious greys and greenish yellows of irises, and all

32. *Campanula lactiflora* 'Loddon Anna'.

the other lovely possibilities. There are other borders where colours have been graded, the cooler colours being reserved for the foreground as one approaches working up to warmer colours like pinks and pale yellows and ending in a blaze of scarlets, gold, and fiery orange. In other borders colours are generally distributed, harmonious groupings being the major consideration. Then there are gardens devoted to single colours. These are usually combined with silver and grey foliage, which are the best foil for blending and accentuating colours. The blue and grey border, the white border, the orange and red border, the pink border, and various others have all been tried. The garden devoted to blues and mauves is greatly improved by the inclusion of silver and soft sulphur and primrose yellow. This brings the border to life. In the same way a little crimson or purple in the pink border takes away the chocolate-box look. I do not advocate one-colour borders unless for some special position or taste. They are harder to bring off successfully because of the limitations, and they belong in large gardens, where all the other colours can be grown elsewhere. One-colour borders usually do not suit a small garden.

There is no doubt that by bringing pale colours to the front the border gains in depth. But this is no reason why the whole margin should be a line of ghosts without a dash of deep rich colour here and there for relief. One of the arguments against groups of equal size throughout a border is the fact that some colours which are very bright may be wanted in small quantity. In painting, a small patch of bright orange or scarlet can bring to life a large canvas, otherwise impeccably painted but dull. This quantitative and qualitative theory of colour is a fascinating one, and when planting scarlet poppies, brilliant fiery *Lychnis chalcedonica*, or crimson paeonies, it is probable that a much smaller clump will suffice to set off the soft blue of anchusas, the delicate glaucous colouring of thalictrums, or the silvery white and creamy yellow of lupins. What this theory really amounts to is that a little of certain colours accomplishes as much as a lot of others, but this is no reason for not having a lot of a colour if you like it.

Lastly, remember when mixing colours that you are gardening primarily to suit yourself. I like magenta and pink together and strong orange and blue-purple. You may not. There are many theories about colours that clash, but there are infinite shades of each, and some of these that probably won't clash. As you gain confidence you can be original and daring if you will, and be successful.

One other point is worth mentioning. The interplanting of different colours of the same plant is often advocated, as, for example, mixing mauve, purple, and plum-coloured phlox or several shades of delphinium. This must be done with care. It is effective in borders where the groups are large, with the result that there are actually groups of the two or three colours running into each other. I wouldn't advocate alternation of single plants

33. *Campanula persicifolia* growing through other plants.

of each colour. Secondly, it is important that the varieties are uniform in their flowering seasons and are of the same height or, failing that, that the tallest end up at the back. On the whole I don't advocate mixing clumps, though where flowers come in a close range of harmonizing colours, like foxgloves or seedlings of the taller campanulas (*C. lactiflora* and *C. latiloba*), the results are excellent, the slight colour variations making a richer group.

Planning for the Individual Requirements of Plants

Besides the aesthetic principles discussed above, there is the practical matter of providing plants with what they require. If there is a shady section in the border as the result of trees or the shadows cast by buildings, advantage should be taken of using plants suited to semi-shade. Here is the place for *Campanula persicifolia* (Plate 33), hellebores, digitalis, bergenias, and *Anemone japonica.* For plants that do well in light, well-drained soil, like romneyas, alstroemerias, *Salvia haematodes*, or *Thermopsis montana*, choose a sunny, well-drained bit. Kaffir lily (*Schizostylis coccinea*), *Lobelia cardinalis* and its lovely varieties, and phloxes want a moister position, which may be provided if one part of the border is lower than the rest. Individual requirements can be provided at planting time by the inclusion of peat and leaf to make the soil more retentive of moisture for certain clumps, chalk or mortar rubble to provide lime for dianthus, and sharp sand around lily bulbs and the fleshy crowns of eremurus to ensure good drainage. More will be said on this matter in the next chapter, but it is included here as it is necessary to take advantage of all existing variations of soil, shade, and moisture when planning.

4 · The Making of the Border

After plans have been drawn up on paper, the next task is to prepare the site for planting. Here the gardener is faced with a variety of problems. If the site has never been under cultivation, as in the case of new gardens, the problem of making a woodland or herbaceous garden will be more difficult than it will be on tilled land, for here the ground will have been dug and the tilth of the soil improved, although it may still leave a lot to be desired. Both will have to be thoroughly cleaned, deeply dug, fed, and levelled.

A special word of warning is due to those who are making borders and beds in the vicinity of new construction. In theory, the builder should have skimmed off the good top-soil to use for surfacing after the rough grading has been done around the house. Unfortunately this is a practice all too often neglected, and top-soil is apt to have been buried under the hard core of poor, unfertile subsoil, brought up from the depths of the foundations. If this is the case, good soil should be brought in from the outside, especially in small town gardens, where such conditions are most likely to exist because of the proximity of the garden to the house.

Cleaning the Soil

It oftens happens that the site selected is badly infested with weeds. This is particularly true of land that has been under cultivation and which during a period of neglect has been over-run with ground elder, bindweed, couch grass, and other invasive perennial weeds. These must be completely removed at all cost, as even a few broken roots will in no time spread through the border, growing into the roots of the flowers. We have all seen the deplorable state of borders in which these weeds became established in the war years. In fact, this plight was the direct cause for the abrupt demise of many a hardy border.

The solutions to weed-infested borders are various, but they all involve hard physical work and often the lapse of considerable time before planting is possible. One method is to dig over the piece of ground two spits deep (a spit is roughly 12 inches or the depth of the blade of the average spade) removing every bit of root, as perennial weeds can survive even at considerable depth, unlike annual weeds, which can be used as green manure if dug in at the bottom of a single spit or even less. On heavy soils the removal of weeds is particularly difficult, as the clods of earth are firm and do not break up as they do on sandy soils or those rich in humus and leaf mould. The action of frost, wind, and rain will in time help to break down the soil, so it is advisable to leave the bed for a winter and re-dig it in early spring, removing any traces of weed remaining. You will be surprised how many there probably are. Often a cleaning crop, such as potatoes, will be advantageous, particularly on soil not previously cultivated, though this will delay the planting of the border for a year. So would the use of sodium chlorate or any of the patented weed-killers, lethal but of course rendering the soil barren for a year. In any case I far prefer the first method of digging and removing every bit of root. The inevitable stray bit that is left can be dealt with later. Another solution is to grow annuals and bedding plants for the first summer.

No matter which solution is chosen a great deal of patience will be required. How often the gardener hears this word – already I have mentioned patience with yew hedges, patience with difficult plants like *Dictamnus albus* and *Campanula lactiflora*, which are slow to establish, and above all patience with the weather.

Types of Soil

Soil may roughly be grouped under the four headings according to its major component: clay, sand and gravel, chalk and lime, and peat. Each has very different properties and requires special methods of cultivation, feeding, and watering. The more you can learn about your particular soil, the better, for it will help with your corrective measures and the selection of plants. A soil analysis to test the degree of acidity or alkalinity measured by a scale of values designated as pH is advisable, and this can be accomplished through the County Agricultural Adviser or The Royal Horticultural Society for their Fellows. There are also small sets for testing at home. The natural flora and even the weeds can tell much as to the type of soil and its fertility.

The term pH is a scale of values which designates the degree of acidity or alkalinity. Acid or sour soils are helped by a liberal application of hydrated lime or basic slag. The latter is particularly suited to acid soils. Both are applied in autumn so that they may act through the winter along with the elements of weather. Lime should be applied at the rate of 4 to 8 ounces per square yard on heavy acid clay and basic slag at 4 ounces per square yard. Do not use either of these in conjunction with manure, as the nitrogen is released too rapidly and wasted. In subsequent years the autumn dressing should probably be more modest and always withheld in areas where lime-haters are planted. The scale of pH values ranges from 1 to 14, with soils below 7 designated as acid, those above being alkaline. Soils in the close vicinity of pH 7 are neutral, and of course are ideal, as they can easily be altered to suit the specialized requirements of any plant, acid or lime-loving. Fortunately with border plants there are few acid-loving plants corresponding to the numerous ericaceous shrubs, including the heathers and enormous rhododendron family. Actually we are not concerned here with soils outside a range of pH 5–8.

CLAY SOIL is heavy, cold, and hard to work. It has a high water table, and because of the fine particles and their special composition water is held in suspension around them, with the result that it is insufficiently aerated and the roots of plants have a difficult time to assimilate nourishment in solution even though there is a sufficiency. This paradoxical situation must be corrected. Very heavy wet borders will require additional drainage by the construction of special drains, but this is a matter that cannot be described here. Our object will be to improve the drainage and aeration of the soil by improving its composition. This can be done by the addition of sharp sand, grit, weathered coal ashes, coarse peat and manure, preferably stable manure with coarse straw. A combination of these will in time make the soil friable so that it can be more easily worked and prevent it from forming a hard surface crust and subsequent cracking as it dries. Clay soil must never be worked in wet weather or when frost is in the ground. It tends to be sour and sometimes acid – apparently a case of redundancy of terms, but the former is used to describe its state of health and the latter its pH value.

SANDY SOILS and those containing coarse grit and gravel tend to be dry and light with a low water table. In summer plants will quickly feel the effects of drought. Light soils are improved by large quantities of humus provided by introducing green manure (weeds, grass mowings, etc.) under the top spit when digging. Very generous quantities of manure, leaf mould, spent hops, and peat greatly increase the water-retaining potential and the soil texture. It must always be remembered that food is absorbed by plants in solution, and both the water and the food must be present. In light soils with a low water table, water drains away very rapidly, taking the food with it, and this must be constantly replaced until the humus content of the soil is sufficient to retain it. Potash is also short in light soils, and must be replaced by balanced fertilizers or by light applications of sulphate of potash. Lime is required and should be applied as ground chalk or marl, as these leach out less quickly than powdered lime.

CHALK AND LIMESTONE SOILS are often berated, but if there is sufficient depth of soil before reaching a solid pan they can be very fertile, and strangely enough they do not dry out too badly. Of course, the range of plants is limited, but with herbaceous plants as mentioned above this is not serious. Good cultivation is necessary, and the addition of humus in any form, especially compost, leaf, peat, and hops, improves the texture and nourishes the soil, while manure is worth its weight in gold. Lime in any form is obviously not required. Ammonium sulphate, which has a very low pH, may be used to counteract excessive alkalinity. Bone meal is less effective on alkaline soils than on neutral ones, as the former are usually rich in calcium phosphate, the principal component of bone meal. Plants on chalk and limestone may suffer from chlorosis, indicated by a yellowing of the leaves and caused by mineral deficiencies, particularly by a shortage of assimilatable iron as the result of the calcium. This may be overcome by the addition of sequestrenes. There is usually a shortage of potash as well, and this can be supplied by a balanced fertilizer or sulphate of potash.

Those who still feel a reluctance to garden on chalk or limestone have only to look at some of the wonderful gardens on the lower slopes of the Sussex Downs or in Dorset and Gloucestershire where these conditions prevail.

PEATY SOILS, which are found in Cornwall, Wales, and the West of Scotland, do not make good herbaceous borders because of excessive acidity and such a high degree of moisture retention that they are often water-logged. Such soils must be heavily drained to let in the air and raise the soil temperature to encourage the action of bacteria to break down the vast accumulation of vegetable matter. The addition of lime to correct the acidity and release locked-up nitrogen is essential. Wood ashes will have a beneficial effect if available in quantity, as they have a pH of 9. Sharp sand, grit, and mortar rubble improve both soil texture and aeration. Peaty soil will require perseverance to render it suitable for herbaceous borders, although it offers excellent opportunities for certain plants which will grow in peaty woodland gardens. Compost, leaf mould, and manure will improve its fertility.

Digging and Feeding

Having settled on a site, pegged out the ground plan, and carefully considered the nature of the soil as to composition, drainage, and fertility, the gardener can start the operations of digging and feeding. I say the operations, as they must go hand in hand if the border is to be successful. Double digging will be necessary, and by this we mean the removal of the top spit of soil and the breaking up of the soil in the bottom spit, at the same time incorporating green manure, turves grass side down, dung, and if necessary even coarse sand to improve drainage. This combined operation will provide for soil suitable for root penetration to a depth of 24 inches, ensure good drainage and a suitably low water table, and provide adequate nourishment, not only for the current year but resources as well for roots to reach out for in subsequent ones. It must always be remembered that the initial deep digging is an

34   35

36   37

Double Digging

34. The soil from the first trench is placed conveniently for filling the last trench.
35. Breaking up the second spit to the full depth of the fork.
36. Covering the broken-up ground of the second spit with manure.
37. Forking manure into second spit.

operation not to be repeated for some years if ever. Although the border will subsequently be replanted, probably it will never be re-dug in its entirety, as plants that resent disturbance, like paeonies, will be left.

When should the border be dug? If the ground is to be made ready for autumn planting, the border should be dug over in early or mid-summer to give it time to settle. If spring planting is contemplated, although this is not generally advised save on cold late soils, then the border should be dug over in the autumn and left for the beneficial action of winter weather to break it down still further. Much will depend on circumstances, and often it is not practical to wait long for the settling process. In this event the soil should be trodden to consolidate it, but only if friable and in good condition. If it is heavy the less it is trodden on the better.

Never dig soil when it is very wet or there is frost coming out of the ground. It will be more difficult and the results will leave much to be desired. The soil will cling to the spade and your shoes. The digging of a border and the planting of it as a spring operation is possible on heavy soils, but even then it is not recommended. On light soils there is danger of spring droughts.

Now for the actual method of digging (Plates 34–7). Work from a higher to lower level, as it is easier to maintain an even surface. Be sure your spade is sharp and clean, scraping it or even washing it if working on sticky clay or chalk. Having established the edge of the border or bed, dig a straight trench across it a foot deep and not more than 2 feet wide. Wheel this soil to a canvas laid on the grass or path at the far end of the border in readiness for the satisfying moment when it will be used to fill the last trench. Now dig over the next spit of soil in the bottom of the trench, breaking it up as much as possible and using a fork if necessary. This soil, of course, is not removed. Annual weeds can be buried in the lower spit, invasive perennials being relegated to the bonfire. Manure should be laid on the top of the now carefully dug second spit to provide deep nourishment for the roots of hungry plants. Now transfer the top spit of the adjoining 2 feet to this carefully prepared sub-soil. This may be enriched by a thin layer of rotted manure, compost, leaf mould, or spent hops scattered over the whole surface and mixed into the top spit as it is transferred to its new position. These additions will depend on individual soil requirements discussed above. Lime may also be needed, although mixing lime and manure is not advocated as a future practice. If well-decomposed dung or the next best manure, a good sweet garden compost, is not available, either because of scarcity or expense, then peat mixed with bone meal, artificial balanced fertilizers, spent hops, shoddy, leaf mould, etc., are suggested substitutes, depending on requirements of the particular soil. This last cannot be over-emphasized, just as it will later be necessary to cater for the tastes of individual plants. This, in fact, is one of the reasons for not using too much lime. It can be added where required later.

The freshly dug ground should now be left to settle, although if immediate planting is necessitated by circumstances it can be consolidated by treading and then a fine surface tilth prepared by raking and levelling.

Conditions and Seasons Propitious for Planting

The moment has at last arrived when the gardener can deal with plants. The best time for planting is usually the autumn. The locality, the nature of the soil, and even the season are cogent factors to be considered, the last so uncertain that it cannot be anticipated. On normal soils in the south and west, and for that matter over a great deal of the country, planting is best completed from late September onwards until mid-October and satisfactory until mid-November or even later in a mild season. Certain plants should definitely be reserved for spring planting, including grey, silver, and woolly-leaved plants, pyrethrums (Plate 38), *Aster amellus*, monardas, romneyas, catananches, gaillardias, and tender plants like penstemons and *Lobelia cardinalis*. At time of planting the soil should be friable and not too moist. Friable soil is crumbly and loose but not dry like dust. The later the time of planting in the autumn, the greater the danger of heavy autumn rains. It must also be remembered that many autumn-flowering perennials, such as heleniums (Plate 39), kniphofias, Michaelmas daisies, and schizostylis, will not be ready for lifting at the end of September, when they will still be in flower. Lastly, on wet soils slugs are active in late autumn and winter.

38. *Pyrethrum*
   'White Madeleine'.

39. *Helenium*
   'Wyndley'.

Spring planting is fraught with dangers. On heavy clay soils the soil will be too heavy to work and the plants will not break into growth for too long a period after transplanting because of the low temperature of the soil. Secondly, in a very early spring the whole schedule is advanced and there may not be time for all the spring jobs, the planting of a border being a major one. Lastly, nurseries are having problems getting plants packed and delivered on time. On the other hand, on newly dug borders or where soil is heavy and low-lying plants may not grow away in autumn and lie all winter subject to cold and damp. In such cases spring is to be preferred, as in towns where there are prolonged fogs. In any case, certain plants can be added in spring to the border largely planted in autumn.

If plants arrive during an autumn or spring drought it may be necessary to saturate the border a day or two before planting and then cultivate it lightly the following day to break up the surface and make it friable. This is particularly true of borders prepared in the summer months.

Laying out the Border

Before unpacking the plants or assembling them from reserve beds, the planting scheme should be transferred from the paper plan to the ground. The complexity of it will dictate the method. The border can be pegged off into blocks of 5 or 10 feet or any convenient unit, depending on its scale. Strings can be used to mark a grid, or certain convenient clumps of plants can be established as guides. A sprinkling of sand is convenient to outline the shape and area of each planting group, and these can in turn be labelled. If sand is not available a line can be drawn with the tip of a trowel or the corner of a hoe. When this has been completed the plants should be unpacked and laid out where they are to be planted (Plate 40). Importance of proper spacing between plants in groups and of the groups themselves must be given special consideration, as is shown in Plate 45 of a border in spring. All the factors of habit, ultimate height and spread, and flowering season must be considered, although these have already been considered when the plan was made and the plants ordered. With most herbaceous plants errors can be rectified at a later date, but some, like paeonies, alstroemerias, and dictamnus, owing to their dislike of disturbance, must be sited correctly from the start.

Directions for Planting

Depth of planting is again important. Plants too deeply embedded, especially in heavy wet soils, are doomed. Shallow planting in light soils, which will tend to settle considerably, can result in equal losses. The nature of the root-stock of the plant and the character of the soil are definite guides. If a plant has a long tap root, like oriental poppies, hollyhocks, verbascums, anchusas, and acanthuses, they should be deeply and firmly planted. Fortunately with such plants the soil level of previous planting can be determined, and if they are planted an inch or so deeper this will allow for the subsequent settling of the soil. Plants with a mass of fibrous roots and numerous growing shoots, like phlox, Michaelmas daisies, pinks, pyrethrums, and *Achillea ptarmica*, must not be deeply planted (Plate 41). This applies particularly to surface rooters, like monardas, *Stachys lanata*, and London pride. Plants with bud growths and root-stocks, like paeonies, dicentra, aconitums, and bocconias, should have their growth buds well covered when planted in autumn.

The size and the shape of the hole will depend on the root development of the plant and its required planting depth. This presents no problems, as the freshly dug soil will be easily shifted with a trowel for smaller plants and a spade for larger ones. As for all plants, it is essential to have enough room to spread out the roots so that they are not curled back upon themselves or twisted. Plate 42 shows a verbascum with its large coarse roots being properly planted in an adequate hole allowing room for the roots to spread and deep enough for the crown to be planted at surface level without twisting of the roots.

If the soil is dry, plants should always be watered or puddled in by filling the hole with water from a can after the plant has been properly set and its roots sprinkled with loose earth. This settles the soil around the roots, tends to draw them down, and assures that water gets to the hair tips of the roots which most require it. By the time the plants in the group or an adjoining one have been planted in this fashion the water will have seeped away and the

40. Plants laid out in groups on prepared bed ready for planting.

41. Fibrous-rooted plants require an ample hole for root spread. Hold plant so that crown is just below surface level and work soil through the roots.

70

42. Planting a fleshy-rooted verbascum. Note depth of hole to make room for massive root system.

43. Scatter loose soil and work it through the roots, then fill the hole with a spade and firm by treading.

44. Firm soil thoroughly with fingers and level off soil so that water does not collect.

holes can be filled with earth and firmed. Be sure not to fill and firm while there is still free water, as it will create a mud pack and bake hard.

The firming of a plant in the ground is important. Larger plants require the pressure of the foot, as demonstrated in Plate 43. Fibrous-rooted plants, and those with delicate roots should be lightly firmed with the fingers (Plate 44). Thoroughness in either case is essential, partly to destroy air pockets, partly to fix the roots in the soil so that the plants will not be loosened by wind activity when they start into growth or be heaved up by winter frosts. The same principles apply to good potting, where firmness is essential. On heavy wet soils firming must be much more gently done as the soil packs. After firming, and especially if the plants have been watered in, the soil should be lightly but thoroughly pricked over to prevent it from forming a hard crust, to discourage capillary attraction, which hastens evaporation, and to level the soil so that no pools are formed in subsequent rains. Moreover, in the course of planting the border was probably heavily trodden and the packed areas also must be broken down.

If borders are sticky it may be necessary to put down planks from which to work (Plate 85).

Certain plants require special conditions for their successful cultivation. Lupins, as we shall see in Chapter 12, dislike lime and manuring. If these are to be planted on chalky soil, then special pockets should be prepared by taking out the soil and adding a large quantity of peat, leaf mould, or hop manure to render the soil more neutral. Pinks do not like heavy acid soil, and it would be necessary to add chalk or marl or mortar rubble as well as sharp sand to improve the drainage. Heavy feeders, like paeonies and delphiniums, can have an extra amount of manure worked into the bottom spit under their roots before planting, and the top spit can be removed and mixed with more well-rotted dung, bone meal, and a little peat. Thus we see it is possible to accommodate most plants. On the other hand, if conditions are not at all suited it may be better to forgo the plant and grow what is happy.

Certain plants may require special treatment after autumn planting. For example, plants like delphiniums and campanulas, particularly attractive to slugs, should be given a top dressing of coal ashes (Plate 84) or sharp sand, while plants that break into growth early, like aconitums, or tender subjects, like *Alstroemeria* Ligtu Hybrids and eremurus, should be given a protection of litter or sand. Plants which have no crowns or remains of stems above ground should be marked with sticks, particularly if they are late in breaking into growth in the spring, as in a new border one has not yet memorized the planting pattern, and guidance is necessary.

Records and Labelling

After the border has been planted there is the question of labels. About this there is considerable difference of opinion. I personally hate obtrusive labels. White-painted wooden labels are too conspicuous. There are also various plastic ones to tie on to the plant or to a cane in the clump, but these are not easy to find, and because of the depth of the border only the labels on front-range plants are readily accessible (Plate 45). Personally, I prefer to rely on the master plan, or to give every group a number, the names being entered in a record book under that number. This works beautifully until alterations start which involve the amalgamation, elimination, or addition of groups. This immediately makes this system unwieldy.

Records should be kept containing lists of plants ordered and their sources. Notes should be made when plants are ordered at flower shows for autumn or spring delivery or on visits to nursery trial grounds and exhibition borders. I, for one, often forget what I have ordered and the quantity, so that there are more new plants than spaces. More will be said regarding other records in subsequent chapters.

Labour-saving Precautions

When digging, planting, or altering the border do not track soil on to grass or gravel paths. Secondly, do not pile earth on grass. If it is left for long it will cause a yellow patch and it is always difficult to clear. Put down canvas, burlap, or even a platform of boards. Similarly, when lifting and dividing plants make use of canvas, matting (Plate 61), or even a wheelbarrow. Any professional gardener trained in the old school will be very emphatic about this. Loose earth on paths ultimately encourages weeds.

During planting operations do not lay out more plants than are to be dealt with immediately. Likewise cover plants after they have been unpacked so that they are not exposed to sun and wind. If they seem dry or if there is to be considerable delay before planting sprinkle them lightly with water and move them to shelter. Usually it is better not to unpack plants if there is to be a delay of a day or two, rather than heeling them in and then lifting again, as they were probably properly packed in anticipation of delay. On the other hand, if a long time has elapsed in transit or if weather is highly unsuitable they can be plunged in moist granulated peat, where they will be safe for a time. During protracted delays they should be lined out carefully and not just dumped in bundles in the ground, as the earth will not settle around the roots, and cold and damp can take their toll.

45. A well-established border in spring showing correct spacing of individual plants, their grouping, and methods of labelling.

5 · Food and Water

Plants, like humans, require both food and water, though fortunately for us they don't require three square meals a day. In the last chapter we have seen how the border was enriched with deep feeding to last for some years when initially prepared. It must be remembered, however, that herbaceous plants are hungry, each year producing a vast amount of stem, leaf, flower, and seed, although the last should be curtailed, as it exhausts the plant and the soil unnecessarily. Owing to the tidy nature of our gardens, nothing goes back naturally into the soil, as happens in woodland or on natural fields and downlands. Nature's normal process of putting back humus is frustrated by our bonfires and rubbish piles. The concentrated drain of crammed herbaceous border on the food reserves is too often under-estimated.

A compost heap is man's answer. Any garden large enough to have an herbaceous border is certainly large enough to boast a compost pile. This should be properly constructed and a few simple fundamental principles followed to ensure a quick result and sweet-smelling light compost. As there are excellent books and pamphlets on this subject, procedure is omitted here. All the annual weeds, dead heads, old stalks, and foliage from the border should end up on the compost pile, and these should be augmented with *thin* layers of grass mowings, dead leaves, and vegetable waste from the kitchen. Fats in any form are taboo. The compost pile will be the source of rich top dressings and special soil for favoured clumps. There are those who say that only organic manures should be used in gardening. There are others who shout about the praises of inorganic fertilizers. What no one denies is the inestimable value of garden compost, not only to feed the soil but also to improve its composition, for, save well-rotted manure, there is nothing more beneficial to light, hungry soil or to thin soils on chalk or limestone strata. In fact, every type of soil is benefited by it.

Later, when we consider the border by seasons, certain feedings will be recommended, but here let us consider the possibilities of what to use and how and when to apply it so that the best results will be obtained. Dung, of course, must head the list. An annual top dressing in autumn of well-rotted manure has no equal substitute. Old farmyard manure is best for this purpose, although stable manure is good on clay soils and puts bulk into very light soils. Poultry manure if available is very good but strong. It must be well aged, and can be applied mixed with spent hops or granulated peat at a rate of not less than seven of the latter to one of manure. Poultry manure makes a wonderful autumn mulch for the lily-of-the-valley bed, and here it can be used at a rate of five to one, or even less if applied late in the autumn. Where there is ample litter mixed with the droppings this dilution is not required.

Compost is the best substitute for manure. It can be used as a top dressing and is very useful to sprinkle through the roots and exposed crowns of plants like phloxes, Michaelmas daisies, pyrethrums, and monardas. With plants that have the tendency to enlarge rapidly by reaching outward, like Michaelmas daisies, physostegias, centaureas, and campanulas, a ring of rich soil around the outside tends to increase their invasive tendencies but feeds them best. New soil or enrichment should be scattered through the centre as well. With plants that tend to work out of the soil or to grow along the ground, like bergenias, heucheras, and *Chrysanthemum maximum*, a little sieved compost or leaf mould tends to cover the sensitive points and encourage root growth until such time as replanting and division are practical.

After the first year or two very heavy feeders, like delphiniums and dahlias, will require extra sustenance if particularly large blooms are desired. Soil may be removed in pockets and dung worked into the bottom spit before replanting in subsequent years. Then with the soil removed a mixture can be made by adding finely chopped manure, bone meal, and granulated peat, this formula being varied to suit special plants. Where manure or compost is not available, a basic fertilizer combining the three elements most needed to stimulate plant growth – nitrates, potash, and phosphates, the last to encourage root growth – may be applied. But never forget the vital necessity of additional humus, which is being removed from the soil by the hungry plants. This must be restored by the addition of granulated peat, hops, chopped bracken, leaf mould, grass mowings, or other forms of vegetable bulk. Peat is the most readily available of these.

As extra nourishment light applications of sulphate of ammonia at the rate of 1 to 2 ounces per square yard scattered among the plants in late spring promote growth and later sulphate of potash in similar proportions encourages free and generous flowering. The latter should be applied at the same rate but at several times in the course of the spring and early summer. On light, sandy soils the amount may be doubled. Apply them evenly and well away from the foliage and crown of the plants, as they have a burning action. Water them in well.

Many perennial plants are not gross feeders. If borders are too heavily manured their growth is leafy and rank. Artemisias, eryngiums, lupins, echinops, valerian, and anaphalis are examples. In the mixed border there are shrubs such as cistus and broom which also respond to a meagre diet.

Feeding in summer with liquid manure is very beneficial. Soak a bag of manure in a tank or water butt. Cow, horse, sheep, or poultry manure is suitable, the last two being particularly strong. After a couple of days remove the liquid as required and dilute until it is the colour of tea. This is most beneficial for plants, and contains far more nutrient than any 'nice cup of tea' for humans, no matter how comforting the latter. It is important that this is applied so that it reaches the roots and does not run off. A ring or collar of earth may be formed around individual plants or clumps to prevent this. Feedings may be repeated at bi-weekly intervals or if the solution is weak and the weather dry at weekly ones.

There are other valuable organic fertilizers, including hoof and horn, dried blood, bone flour, and bone meal. Dried blood is an excellent food, and may be applied neat or in solution. Several ounces may be soaked in a watering-can overnight and then applied like liquid manure. Other organic fertilizers include guano, fish manure, and sludge. These like bone meal, or the more readily assimilable bone flour, should be scattered over the surface and then hoed into the top 2 inches of soil. Dried fertilizers should be applied on a still day, as they tend to blow about badly. Remember that bone meal is not a complete fertilizer, as it is low in potassium and nitrogen, its principal use being as a source of phosphates and calcium. It is a long-term fertilizer, and the coarser it is, the less quickly it will be assimilated or leached out of the soil. Applications of 4 ounces per square yard are advised.

Watering

As mentioned in Chapter 4, newly planted perennials should be watered to settle the soil around their roots unless the bed is very moist. Likewise we have seen that applications of fertilizers in powdered form, whether organic or inorganic, should be worked into the top of the soil and watered in.

All herbaceous borders will go through dry periods. On light, dry soils and in sunny, well-drained positions plants dry out more quickly than on those of a heavier nature. Familiar flagging of foliage and flowers in hot sunshine is the first sign, followed by yellowing of leaves, stunted growth, and a lack of flower as the drought continues. Heavy dew at night will temporarily revive the flagging leaves, but the scorching sun the next day continues its exhausting process. Spells of dry weather are usually associated with summer, but in recent years protracted spells of spring drought coupled with drying winds have done untold damage. This is particularly true of newly planted borders where there is insufficient moisture to enable adequate root action.

Obviously, corrective measures must be taken despite the very staunch supporters of the non-watering school. If water is available either from the main or from wells and no restrictions have been imposed as to its use, then I am all for watering. It must be done *properly*, 'properly' being considered synonymous with 'thoroughly'. Herein lies the secret. Sprinkling the surface, especially with a coarse spray, only aggravates the trouble, drawing the hair roots to the surface and making subsequent flagging inevitable. It is true, of course, that even wetting the foliage helps to revive plants (witness the effects of a night's dew on drooping leaves), but the kind of watering that really helps is a good thorough soaking that sinks in deep and reaches the roots. The results are identical to those of a two-day gentle rain, not those of

46. Watering a bed of dahlias with a patented sprayer.

a violent downpour that accompanies a thunderstorm, as it runs off the surface of the soil, collecting in the hollows or ending up in the drains and culverts. To enable watering to be effective, break up the surface soil, especially if there is a crust, and when the soil has begun to dry out a few hours after the storm, again go over the surface with a hoe or pronged hand cultivator to prevent rapid transpiration.

Artificial watering (Plate 46) should simulate prolonged gentle rain. If a border is given such a soaking it will survive for a week or more without further attention save in very hot, dry soils. A sprinkling system with a rotator and a fine spray is ideal. It should be allowed to play on a given area until the water has penetrated to a depth of at least 2 or 3 inches, preferably more. Where the water supply is not sufficient for overall watering, then it should be reserved for those plants requiring it, any plants like artemisias, anthemis, eryngiums, echinops, gypsophilas, and verbascums surviving either because of their limited requirements or their deep roots, which tap the lower water level. Selected clumps can be watered by hand, a rim of soil having first been banked up like a crater around each plant or group to hold a pool until it has soaked into the roots. In this way phloxes, monardas, delphiniums, and platycodons can be given a new lease of life. A few hours later scratch up the surface of the soil between the plants to ensure a good tilth, which minimizes capillary action.

Watering should be done in the late afternoon or evening if time allows, but if there is a long border the sprinklers may have to run through the daylight hours. In spite of theories to the contrary, this does no actual harm, and in many hot, dry countries where conditions are extreme and the sun fierce, watering continues around the clock without damage to the plants. Recently various devices have appeared, including limp plastic tubing with a series of tiny holes. This is laid on the surface of the soil, coiling through the particular clumps or areas where water is required. The water seeps into the soil without spraying the foliage. This method is slow but thorough. Other similar devices have been produced.

Again I make the plea – water thoroughly and intelligently. Wet earth and glistening plants after a light spray in the cool of the evening please the eye, but such casual sprinkling will not correct the cause of the trouble. Watering should not be confused with syringeing or spraying to wash foliage, such as is practised in many town gardens with excellent results but with a different objective, namely to clean the leaves.

Where watering is impossible for various reasons, including the primary fact that there may be no one to tend the hose, mulches to retain the moisture in the soil are recommended. This is not a method of putting moisture back into the soil but of preserving what is there by minimizing evaporation and transpiration. This fundamental concept must be fully comprehended. The mulch consisting of peat, grass mowings, or spent hops should be applied when the soil is still moist. If the ground has already begun to dry, thoroughly soak it, or the mulch will be to little purpose. Next reduce the surface to a good tilth, first scattering a light application of bone meal or dried blood if the border requires feeding. Then the mulch should be spread over the surface to the depth of several inches. Peat should be applied damp, or it will act as a sponge drawing the remaining surface moisture out of the sod. Grass mowings, in particular, should be scattered thinly. It must be remembered that mulches, especially of mowings will harbour slugs and preventive measures must be taken (see p. 135). It should also be realized that mulches tend to keep the moisture in the soil but by the same token keep the rain out. If the dry spell breaks it may be advisable to remove the mulch or work it into the soil, and by 'break' I do not mean at the sight of the first dark cloud on the horizon.

47. A section of a well-staked border with patented plant supports visible at lower left.

6 · Supporting and Tying

This subject is so important to the appearance of any garden scheme involving herbaceous plants (Plate 47) that I have devoted a whole chapter to it. No matter how beautiful plants may be or how well grown, staking improperly done ruins their effect. It is true, of course, that healthy, vigorous plants will support themselves better than weak ones. Sun-loving plants grown in too shady a spot are among the worst offenders, as they become drawn and attenuated. It also should be realized that plants in a new border will need far more staking than in an established one, first, because growth is not as strong; and second, because plants are small and do not support each other, while the groups in turn are too sparse to buttress each other.

There are two fatal errors prevalent in the supporting of plants, summed up by the phrase 'too little, too late'. Never was this old adage more true. If a plant once grows with a kink in the stem it never looks right no matter how carefully it is staked and tied. If a gale or a torrential rain knocks down the lupins, delphiniums, or hollyhocks, they never recover their full beauty. There is always the temptation to delay staking because of the pressure of other chores, but there are few tasks more urgent. Staking must be done early not only from the point of view of looks but of efficiency as well. If twigging with pea sticks is used, these must be inserted so that the plant literally grows up through them. They must not be pushed among developed stems.

So far I have considered only the 'too late' aspect. The 'too little' half of the maxim is equally applicable. There is a tendency to use too light canes, too little twigging, too few sticks, and not enough ties. The process of supporting plants must be thorough as well as timely. There are many excellent plants that do not require staking, many of them species, and these should be widely used as they help to support others.

On the basis of what I have said, the gardener might well turn his garden into a forest of canes and leafless pea sticks in April.

Nothing is uglier than obvious unconcealed staking. Inevitably, no matter what method is used there will be an ugly period when the supports are much in evidence. Try to have this period as short as possible. If they are inserted when plants are growing rapidly it is amazing how quickly they are concealed, and as soon as the stakes have served their purpose they should be removed.

No fixed time can be laid down for staking the border. The work can be done over a period of time, certain plants like anchusas and oriental poppies requiring attention well in advance of the heleniums and solidagos. However, in many gardens today staking is treated as an operation and the whole border is given its supports at the same time, more being added as other plants mature, these on the whole being relatively few. It is difficult to lay down an exact time, as it will vary from year to year and with different localities. However, staking of early flowers should take place in late April or early May. This will include *Geranium ibericum* and *G. grandiflorum*, paeonies, and delphiniums, as well as the poppies and anchusas mentioned above. The balance of the staking can be delayed until mid-May, when new growth is active and the bare sticks will quickly be concealed.

There are various types of supports. The most common is twigging, also known as pea sticks or pea brush. Then there are bamboo canes, chestnut stakes, metal hoops, and other ingenious devices consisting of grids or coarse meshes supported on folding metal frames. These last are similar in effect to using coarse wire netting fastened to stakes driven into the ground. The type employed will depend largely on the nature of the garden, the size of clumps, and cost. This last can become a very large item in a long border, and obviously in many localities it is far cheaper to cut pea sticks than to buy bamboo canes or metal supports. Let us consider each in turn.

Pea sticks can be cut in winter or very early spring and stacked. The best material is twiggy growth of beech, hornbeam, birch, or alder. Poplar is apt to sprout in wet weather. Supplies of different lengths should be gathered or purchased so that plants of different heights ranging from 1 to 4 feet are provided for. Insert the sticks when the plants are growing vigorously, arranging them through the middle of the group as well as around the outside. The sticks

48. A paeony staked with birch pea sticks interwoven at the top.

should be long enough so that ultimately the flower-heads and the few inches of leafless stem bearing them will stand free but the bulk of the plant has a framework. Twigs can be interwoven and extra long ones bent over into the centre (Plate 48). Twigs are particularly good for plants with a multitude of stems, like paeonies, asters, heleniums, erigerons, salvias, veronicas, and artemisias. They are not suitable for plants with strong, unbranching spikes, like hollyhocks, eremuri, or delphiniums, save for the shorter belladonna types. Plate 49 shows a border at Wisley with twigging in place in mid-May. Plate 50 shows the same section of border four weeks later. Note how the front-line plants need no staking and how in many clumps twigging has completely disappeared, as in the flowering clump of thalictrum in the left centre. Plate 51 shows a similar border in August.

49. A border staked with pea sticks in early May before rapid growth has commenced.

50. The same border a month later in early June with sticks largely concealed.

51. A similar border, well staked with pea sticks, in early August.

Wire attached to pegs set in the ground is another method. A coarse mesh, $1\frac{1}{2}$ to 2 inches, stretched across a bed or border at a distance of a foot to 18 inches from the ground will provide support for wiry-stemmed plants with smallish leaves. It is not suitable for very coarse-leaved subjects. Pyrethrums, coreopsis, scabious, and such plants are well suited. The wire can be painted green and, if put in place over the growing plants just as they reach the height at which the wire is to be fixed, it is soon screened by leaves and flowers. After flowering the wire may be removed and saved for the next season. This method is best applied to beds of one or two varieties rather than to the large mixed border. It is, of course, not adequate for large plants like delphiniums, hollyhocks, and lactucas.

Semicircles of iron with pointed uprights bent from a continuous piece of metal rod are very useful (Plate 52). They should be made in various sizes for different plants. When painted green they become almost invisible when tucked under a plant, either singly or in pairs, to support the weight of a paeony, thermopsis, or baptisia with their spreading, shrubby habit or even taller plants like *Artemisia lactiflora*. The stakes can be driven into the ground to whatever depth required and then raised as the plants grow taller. They are also useful for plants against walls.

Other supports such as metal or wire grids on collapsible legs are very efficient and are best painted dark green. These are available in various shapes and sizes, circular, square, and rectangular (Plate 53). They too can be regulated as to height by raising or lowering them in the ground. They are relatively expensive, but they can be used year after year, and a border in which they are employed can be faultlessly staked (Plate 2).

Plants like delphiniums (Plates 54, 55), eremuri, and galtonias are best staked with bamboo canes. With some plants a single cane is suggested for each spike, not less than three-quarters the height of the stem. It is inserted behind the stem and then secured by a series of ties with raffia, bast, or string. The cane must be securely embedded in the soil so that it cannot pull out and of sufficient height that the truss of flowers is supported. If too short canes are used, the stem often snaps at the base of the flower spike. Sometimes it is possible to tie three or four stems to the same cane

52. A type of plant support useful either singly or in pairs for large plants like paeonies and shrub roses.

or stake if it is implanted near to the clump. Then the various stalks growing out from the root are secured to the central stake by multiple ties. Bocconias, verbascums (Plate 56), Michaelmas daisies, thalictrums, and sidalceas are among the plants that can be treated in this way.

Other plants will require a series of canes. Often it is possible to distribute them in and around the clump. Then a criss-cross of green twine is carried around and through the clump, using the canes as a frame. This interlace should be started fairly close to the ground, say 15 to 18 inches, depending on the subject and repeated higher up as required. As the foliage expands, the canes and twine will be concealed. Heavier plants, like dahlias, compositae with massive clusters of flowers, and hollyhocks, may require a stake, preferably of oak, chestnut, or larch, of stouter dimensions to support the weight of the plants. Such stakes will also be invaluable for brooms and old roses in the mixed border.

The test of good staking is that it is practically invisible. When the border is in bloom the stakes and twigs must not be in evidence (Plate 2). Plants must never have a tied-in look, with bulges above and below like a tightly belted figure. Staking must be done well in advance of the time when it will be required, and personal knowledge of the degree of exposure to winds of the site and the characteristic growth of plants on the particular soil will be of assistance. Lastly, much can be done with stakeless plants like *Sedum spectabile, Dictamnus albus, Achillea taygetea, Anemone*

53. Wire plant supports of different shapes show up in this border where erigerons were unfortunately stunted by prolonged drought.

54. Delphiniums well staked, although for windy positions even longer canes are advised.

55. An individual stem of delphinium tied to a cane with a double loop.

56. Well-staked verbascums.

91

57. Columbines require little if any staking.

hupehensis, (*A. japonica*), valerians, columbines (Plate 57), knipho-fias (Plate 58), most phloxes, and tradescantias, to mention only a few. Where there is a choice between a species or variety that requires staking and one that does not, choose the latter in preference.

Far too little has been done to date with the training of herbaceous plants. Recently I was much impressed by the sturdy compact habit of plants like *Artemisia* 'Silver Queen' and *Salvia superba* in a well-known garden, as these plants were superior to those in other gardens. The reason lay in the fact that the growing tips had been removed from time to time to keep the plant from becoming too tall and, in the case of foliage plants like many of the artemisias, from flowering. This same system of stopping can be used with the taller heleniums and golden rods if it is done in time. Michaelmas daisies offer a wide field for experiment. Ver-bascums like 'Gainsborough', 'Pink Domino', 'Bridal Bouquet' and the various 'Cotswold' varieties, can be similarly treated, as it makes them more branching and the tall central spike is lost. In smaller gardens, where this height is not required, lovely effects

58. *Kniphofia* 'Royal Standard', like most kniphofias, requires no staking.

59. A well-cared-for border where plants, including artemisias, have been pinched back to encourage compact growth.

can be produced. Stopping tends to make the flowering season slightly later. Anchusas like 'Opal', 'Pride of Dover', and 'Morning Glory' can also be stopped when the flower stalk has formed by removing the very tip. This encourages lateral branching and makes more compact plants. With the appearance of the new and rather more dwarf varieties 'Royal Blue' and 'Loddon Royalist' this practice is no longer necessary in the smaller garden. The training of perennials is an interesting pastime for the gardener, and with experiment and experience much can be accomplished. Plate 59 shows clumps of silvery artemisias and veronicas along the front of a border which have been carefully pinched back to make them bushy and compact. In this same connexion continuous flowering or copious second bloom can be induced by careful deadheading or cutting back, a discussion of which appears on p. 123.

7 · The Propagation of Hardy Herbaceous Plants

No group of plants is easier to propagate than herbaceous ones, and the methods are various, including division, layering, cuttings, and of course seeds. Grafting on to root-stock is also possible, as in the case of some paeonies and garden varieties of gypsophila like 'Rosy Veil', 'Bristol Fairy', and the double pink 'Flamingo', but this last practice is chiefly restricted to nurseries and need not concern us here. Propagation of the majority of herbaceous plants in our gardens is so easy that after stock plants have been obtained during the initial planting of the border the average gardener should be able to build up sufficient stocks for future replanting and for his further needs, as well as those of close friends. Patience, knowledge of basic principles, facilities such as a cold frame or two, and either time or outside labour are essential. A small greenhouse and a potting shed are very useful but not absolutely necessary.

I have mentioned time as a prerequisite. When propagating plants there are stages which require daily attention. Pans of seeds and newly pricked-out seedlings, for example, must never dry out, while cuttings must be kept moist and, according to one school of thought, at the same time must have occasional air so that they do not damp off. Another school advocates constant moisture in a closed frame or polythene covering. Soft-wood cuttings must be taken at the correct time, properly prepared and inserted. All this is time-consuming and demands regular attention at certain seasons of the year.

The method of propagation to be used will often largely be dictated by the nature of the plant. First there is the question of whether it will come true from seed. If it is a species (i.e., a plant which exists in nature and reproduces itself so that it is identical to the parent or close to it) seed is an excellent means. Examples of species include *Erigeron mucronatus*, *Linum narbonense*, and the Christmas rose *Helleborus niger*. On the other hand, if the plan its a garden hybrid, in most cases man-made, like the wonderful modern phloxes, lupins, erigerons, delphiniums, and hemerocallis, it is probable that the results from a batch of seed from a single pod would be very mixed in colour, habit, size of flower, and scent. In fact, there may not be a single plant that resembles the parent. To illustrate, a seed pod of the charming day lily 'Pink Damask' might well yield a large number of orange, yellow, and nondescript reds and not a single clear pink. In addition, the majority of the flowers may be lacking in symmetry, substance of petal, stamina, and the other attributes of this lovely cultivar. Often plants appear in gardens that are not man-made but distinct breaks or sports. A well-known example is the white *Anemone hupehensis* 'Honorine Jobert', which appeared as a sport of a pink-flowered plant. Such plants and horticultural cultivars must generally be reproduced vegetatively, that is by growing on a piece of the parent plant, by using a bit of the root, stem, or even leaf.

Some cultivars of perennials will come relatively true from seed, or the slight variations resulting will not detract from the effectiveness of the plants when massed, as is the case with many annuals. Good examples are polyanthus, delphinium, and alstroemeria. In the first case the relatively new and very popular blues can be grown from seed and the plants resulting, though not uniform, are attractive in combination and fairly close. The Pacific Strain of delphiniums which are so fine again are offered as strains – whites, blues, pinks, etc., having been segregated. This term strain is a good one, for it means a race of plants with certain fixed characteristics, although there may be colour variation. *Alstroemeria* Ligtu Hybrids is another case in point and is a strain including fine pinks and salmons among the oranges. Strains of *Campanula lactiflora* are attractive if grown from seed, as there is a pleasing play of colours.

The structure of a plant very often indicates the best method of propagation. Plants with fibrous roots and multiple stems, like Michaelmas daisies (Plate 62), phloxes and heleniums, lend themselves to division. Rhizomatous plants, like bearded irises (Plate 138), *Peltiphyllum peltatum*, and lilies of the valley, cry out for division. Others with heavy, thick roots, like day lilies, verbascums

60. The giant cotton thistle is best sown *in situ*.

(Plate 42), anchusas, acanthuses, and oriental poppies, obviously lend themselves to root cuttings or root divisions. Delphiniums, lupins, and penstemons are ideal for stem cuttings and border carnations for layering. The novice must learn the idiosyncrasies of certain plants which do not like to be moved or survive only if divided at a certain season, their requirements as to soil, rooting mediums, and periods required for rooting. The rest will depend on his innate skill, gradual accumulation of experience, and powers of observation.

Seed Sowing. This operation is so widely performed in all types of gardening that great detail is uncalled for here. The time of sowing will depend on the nature of the plant. Many perennials and biennials for that matter should be sown in spring or early summer, especially if they are to be sown outdoors. Lupins, delphiniums, coreopsis, foxgloves, anthemis, and columbines sown in April and May can be transplanted into their final flowering positions in early autumn or spring and will flower their second summer. A few perennials are best sown *in situ*. The handsome giant cotton thistle *Onopordon acanthium*, which associates so well with shrubs or is striking in the silver and grey garden (Plate 60), should be so treated, waiting until the soil is warm in April. It is far easier to sow directly in the ground than to prepare pots or boxes, prick out, etc.

Other seeds are best sown as soon as they are ripe. These include meconopsis, polyanthus, many *Primula* species, astrantia, trollius, and armeria. With meconopsis this is particularly important for good germination. Others, like paeony seeds, need to be exposed to freezing to hasten germination.

The seed bed outside should be in a warm, sheltered spot. The soil should be well prepared and the surface tilth as fine as possible. If the soil is very loose, firm it by treading and then restore the fine surface tilth. If the soil is heavy it should be lightened with a little granulated peat, coarse sand, or leaf mould worked into the surface. Seeds may be sown in drills not more than $\frac{1}{2}$ inch deep, depending on the size of the seeds, and then lightly covered and firmed with the back of a hoe or rake. Finer seeds should be lightly scattered and a little fine soil sieved over it before firming. It may be necessary to cover the seed bed with wire or branches if the birds are active, but usually there are too many other distractions for them to make this necessary. The seed should be lightly watered in if there is a dry spell and seedlings should be kept reasonably moist. Weeds soon choke seed beds. Therefore remove the worst of them, being careful that too many seedlings don't come up with the weeds.

Seeds may also be sown in a similar fashion in a cold frame. With very fine seed this has a great advantage, as the bed can be covered during heavy rain, all watering being done with a can with a fine rose. Seedlings can also be protected against frost. Delicate seeds or plants required early are best sown in pans or boxes as early as February or early March. Pans or boxes must be thoroughly cleaned and then crocked with a light covering layer of coarse leaf, bits of root, fibre, or turf. Fill the container with a seed compost mixed in accordance with the John Innes formula:

2 parts medium loam
1 part leaf or peat
1 part coarse sand
$1\frac{1}{2}$ ounces superphosphate
$\frac{3}{4}$ ounce chalk or limestone

In mixing compost all parts are by bulk unless weight is indicated. This compost can be purchased ready mixed from horticultural suppliers.

The firming of the soil in pots and boxes is very important. For the latter a smooth square of wood $\frac{1}{2}$ inch thick or more with a handle attached to the top is useful, as it packs the soil evenly and firmly, especially along the edges and in the corners. The compost should be moist but crumbly. If it is dry the best plan is to moisten it the night before so that the peat and leaf have time to absorb the water.

Seeds should be sown thinly and evenly, covered with a dusting of sieved compost, and lightly firmed with the soil rammer or the base of another flower-pot. Large seeds, like paeonies or baptisias, can be inserted in the soil to greater depth. Now the seeds should be watered, but, as overhead watering tends to wash out the seeds and float them on the surface, place the pots in a tank or sink and raise the water level to the rim of the pots. When the surface changes colour as the result of the absorbed moisture, remove the pots to a shelf and cover with paper, glass, or muslin. Germination periods differ from a few days to weeks, and in a few cases, as with some paeonies, months or even the following year. Where germination is very long the pots should be sunk in a frame outside.

The tiny seedlings must be carefully watched and watered. As soon as they are large enough to handle they should be pricked out into boxes or frames filled with John Innes Potting Compost No. 1, great care being taken not to damage the hair roots. A small dibber should be used to make the holes and the seedling suspended in the hole while the soil is gently pressed around it. A hardening-off process is essential to enable them to become acclimatized to outside conditions. The seedlings should be gradually exposed to the open air for longer periods each day. When this process has been completed, after a period of several weeks, they can be planted in their permanent homes or into sheltered beds in the kitchen garden to grow until they are needed.

DIVISION. This method is the most common means of vegetative propagation. When clumps become too thick, or when more plants are required the stock should be lifted (Plate 61), the earth removed from the roots, and the plants torn apart (Plate 62). With many plants this will be an easy matter, especially with fibrous, shallow-rooting plants. Monardas, Michaelmas daisies, artemisias, solidagos, and anthemis are good examples. The old, exhausted roots, especially those in the centre, should be discarded, the young, vigorous plants being retained (Plate 63). Spring is generally the preferable season for this operation, and it is essential with pyrethrums, *Chrysanthemum maximum*, scabious, and *Aster amellus* cultivars like 'King George', 'Sonia', and 'Mauve Beauty'. Plates 64 and 65 show the division of bergenias and the preparation of a growth for planting.

Other plants, like day lilies, hostas, agapanthuses, and paeonies, will be difficult to pull apart if long established, and they can be pried apart with two forks (Plates 66 to 68), and cut with a spade or with a sharp knife, as for irises.

Early flowering plants, like trollius, pulmonarias, mertensias, and doronicums, are best divided in early autumn so that they have time to make good root growth before spring. Others, like polyanthus, forms of *Primula juliae*, epimediums, and bearded irises, are best divided immediately after flowering. If the weather is hot and dry they will, of course, require watering until established. Removal of some of the foliage will help, especially with irises by cutting them off about 9 inches from the ground. Paeonies are best divided in late September or October. Many tough plants, like heleniums, solidago, geraniums, bocconia, potentillas, geums, and lysimachias, can be divided either in autumn or spring. Others, like pyrethrums and *Aster amellus*, are best divided in spring, allowance of course always being made for special climates and soils.

61. A clump of Michaelmas daisies lifted for division. Note use of mat to keep grass clean.

62. Tearing apart the fibrous crowns.

63. Division completed. Note old stock for discard on right.

64. A lateral growth of bergenia being severed from the parent plant.

65. The fleshy rhizomatous root ready for shallow planting.

Generally speaking, tap-rooted plants, like eryngiums, anchusas, and poppies, do not lend themselves to division, root cuttings being more satisfactory.

CUTTINGS. These can be differentiated into stem, root, and leaf, although the last hardly concern us here. Cuttings can further be differentiated as soft and half-ripened. The former are

66. Division of hem-
erocallis with two
forks placed back
to back.

67. The clump divided in two by forcing the forks apart.

68. Young healthy
    divisions suitable
    for planting.

soft shoots of new growth, such as those of delphiniums, phloxes, and lupins, taken in early spring. The latter are half-ripened shoots of plants, like penstemons, dianthus, *Lobelia cardinalis*, and *Phygelius capensis*, taken in late summer. These if possible should not be flower-bearing. Cuttings may be taken with or without a heel (a bit of the old wood or root at the base). Delphiniums and lupins are usually taken with a heel (Plate 142) in early spring when the plants are breaking into growth, plants often being lifted and brought into the greenhouse to hasten this process. Other plants, like dahlias, chrysanthemums, *Lobelia cardinalis*, and *Salvia patens*, are lifted in the autumn, wintered in a frame, and then stooled in a greenhouse or warm place in early spring. Soft cuttings can also be copiously induced by cutting back certain plants, such as anthemis, nepeta, and dianthus, after flowering, although with the last do not cut back into old wood. This will ensure an adequate supply of plants for the next spring, as on heavy soils nepeta and pinks are not always reliable. Cuttings taken in late summer or early autumn, of plants such as penstemons and lobelias, are best potted up after they have rooted and placed in a frame for the winter, as they need winter protection (Plate 69).

Cuttings should be carefully selected, only clean, sturdy growths being suitable. Nodal cuttings (those taken just below a stem joint) are preferable to inter-nodal cuttings, as the tissues heal

69. Rooted cuttings of penstemons being stored in a cold frame for the winter.

more quickly, forming scar tissue which seals the cutting. The nodes in chrysanthemums, dianthus, and dahlias are readily visible. It will probably be necessary to remove the lower leaves to make for easy insertion. Cuttings vary in length from 2 to 4 inches. Do not make them too long.

Rooting hormones may be used, but they are not essential. Although they tend to speed up the root formation, they do not ensure the rooting of difficult plants. Rules prescribed by the manufacturer should be closely adhered to, as an excess of hormones can injure the tissues.

Cuttings may be inserted singly or around the edge of a pot (Plates 73, 75) or in boxes. The compost usually consists of sharp sand or a mixture of sifted loam, fine peat, and sharp sand, in the proportions 1, 2, 3 – sand for drainage, peat to hold the moisture, and a small amount of loam to feed the newly formed roots. Pure sand or sand with a little fine leaf or peat drys out very quickly and has no nourishment for the rooted cuttings, which must therefore be potted up quickly in a proper compost. The balanced compost with loam ensures that the cuttings can become well established before disturbance. Make the holes with a small stick or dibber and insert the cutting to the depth of half an inch to an inch or even more, depending on the length of the cutting.

After watering in the cuttings to settle the compost firmly around their stems, move the pots or boxes to a moist atmosphere and shield from the sun. A closed propagating frame is, of course, ideal, and if this is available the cuttings can be inserted into the bed of the frame direct. Bell jars, a box covered with a sheet of glass, or a cold frame are suitable. Keep the cuttings evenly moist. Some gardeners still prefer to wipe off excessive moisture due to condensation daily, but this is less and less the accepted practice. If the cuttings are in a tightly closed frame, they may be given a little air each day, but again this is now not generally thought necessary. Polythene film may be used as a covering for cuttings, as it allows the intake of air but retains all moisture. The basic principle with cuttings is to provide conditions which ensure that they heal and eventually root before too much moisture is lost from the leaves and stem. Cuttings take anywhere from ten days to six weeks to root, hard-wood cuttings of trees and shrubs often taking far longer.

When the cuttings have rooted they may be potted up singly or in boxes and placed in frames to be hardened up before planting out. If they are cuttings taken in late summer or early autumn they will need winter protection.

Let us follow through the entire process of growing dahlias from cuttings. Plate 70 shows the stock tubers growing in a stool bed under glass. Plate 71 shows the selection and cutting of strong shoots with a sharp knife. In Plate 72 note that the cuttings are nodal, the incision having been made just below a pair of leaves, which have been stripped off to allow easy insertion. Plate 73 shows the insertion of the cutting and firming of the compost around it, leaving the soil level about an inch from the rim of the pot to ensure room for watering. In Plate 74 we see well-rooted cuttings being potted on into number 48 pots three weeks later.

Plates 75–7 show similar stages in the propagation of chrysanthemums.

ROOT CUTTINGS. These provide an easy means of propagation of herbaceous plants with large roots of a fleshy, solid nature. The list of suitable subjects includes anchusas, oriental poppies, crambe, acanthus, catananche, *Anemone japonica*, and *Brunnera*

70. Dahlias planted in greenhouse with gentle heat to encourage growths for cuttings.

71. Severing cuttings with a sharp knife.

107

72. Cuttings ready for insertion with lower leaves removed.

73. Firming the cuttings in their pots. Note soil level.

74. Potting-on well rooted cuttings into 5-in. pots several weeks later.

75. Cuttings of chrysanthemums inserted around the edge of a pot. Note crocking and layer of rough material in pots to right.

76. Chrysanthemum cuttings ready for potting.

77. Firming soil carefully with the fingers to avoid root damage.

109

78. The thick roots of a verbascum washed clean preparatory to taking root cuttings.

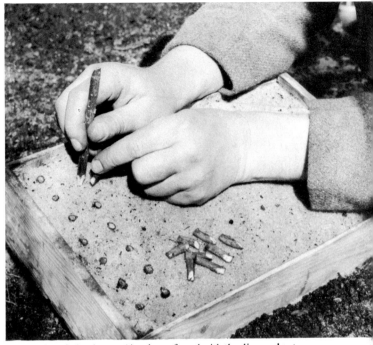

79. Cuttings being inserted in a box of sand with the diagonal cut downwards.

macrophylla. The cuttings can be taken at any time, although early spring and summer seem to give best results. Lift the plants, wash the roots clean, and select solid, active roots (Plate 78). Cut the firm roots into sections 1½ to 2 inches in length, slanting the cut at the base of the root. With a dibber insert the cutting in its proper position as shown in Plate 79 in a box or pot of sandy compost. The cuttings will in time root and send up a growth shoot. They should be potted on or boxed in the same manner as other cuttings. Again they must never be allowed to dry out, and the same hardening process is advised. Root cuttings are used widely in nurseries, new phloxes and other scarce plants being propagated in this fashion.

80. On the right a shoot with slit on under side of stem at a node. On the left a similar shoot after layering.

LAYERING. This method of propagation is only practical with a few perennials, border carnations being the principal one. A long shoot is selected and about 6 or 7 inches from the growing tip a slit (Plate 80) is made on the under half of the stem. This is then pegged down with a forked stick or staple of wire, covered with sifted soil, and watered (Plate 80). The partially severed shoot continues to receive sap from the parent plant, and roots gradually form at the cut. When these are well established the stem should be severed between the plant and the rooted shoot (Plate 82). The new plant can now be lifted. During dry weather the soil must be kept moist to ensure that the wounded stem does not dry out.

Taking leaf cuttings does not concern us here, as it is much more a practice with hot-house plants like begonias, streptocarpus, and saintpaulias. Root grafting, as stated before, is primarily a commercial practice, and again does not warrant description here.

81. At left a rooted plant with another potential layer. At right a
   well-rooted layer with stem from parent plant still attached.

82. Severing a rooted layer.

8 · The Four Seasons

It is hard to know whether to start the cycle with autumn or spring, so much depending on when the annual overhaul is to take place. This must be determined by the locality, the nature of the soil, and personal preference. Since the annual overhaul is of such importance that the year hinges on it, let's weigh the pros and cons of autumn and spring. The time for the major overhaul that is required every three to four years can be settled at the same time.

Autumn is a logical time for these operations, as the garden can be tidied up along with the lawns and kitchen garden so that all is ship-shape for winter. Staking is removed, herbaceous plants are cut to the ground, encroaching clumps lifted, and the sites manured and re-dug. Clashing colours are re-grouped and the border put in readiness for spring. Weather is generally good and there is less pressure of work than in spring. On the other hand, there is a school of thought which claims that it is better not to cut most perennials to the ground in autumn, as the stalks prevent moisture and frost from easy access to the roots and new shoots. Furthermore, more plants move and divide better in spring than in autumn. Lastly, on cold, wet soils plants that have been moved may not make sufficient root growth before cold weather and lie dormant. Yet there is the danger of late spring rains, which make the border unworkable until late in the season, and of prolonged spring droughts, which take such a toll on newly planted perennials. Furthermore, there is the pressure of work in spring, when roses and shrubs must be pruned, vegetables started, lawns raked and rolled, and all the other tasks done. In the final analysis the decision of autumn or spring renovation must be decided on conditions.

In previous chapters I have dealt with the operations of staking, feeding, and propagation, so that it is now possible to sketch the work of the seasons fairly briefly.

Autumn in the border is a lovely time, yet one is impatient to

83. *Lobelia cardinalis* stored in a frame for the winter months.

get on with the work and tidy up for winter. Plants that are to be divided or moved should be dealt with as early as possible after September 1st so that they will have time to settle down before cold weather. Obviously autumn-flowering asters, golden rods, chrysanthemums, anemones, and physostegias must be left to finish blooming. The first frosts will take the dahlias, but others will linger on for a bit. Penstemons which are not hardy, *Salvia patens* and *Lobelia cardinalis* (Plate 83) and *fulgens* varieties, should be lifted and transferred to a box of earth in a cellar or a cold frame. Dahlias should be lifted, the roots cleaned and stored.

All areas in the border where plants are removed should be manured, fed, and prepared, in accordance with the nature of the soil, before replanting. Remove all stakes and plant supports, storing those which can be used a second year. Remove all rubbish and debris which may harbour slugs during the winter months. This argument is a cogent one for cutting perennials down in autumn, although 3 or 4 inches of stalk must be left. This stubble protects the roots and acts as a guide to the location of plants after the border has been cleared. If there are any shrubs at the back of the border these should be cared for as required. Place a late autumn mulch around those plants which need feeding, avoiding plants like scabious, artemisias, echinops, lupins, and the like, which are better on simple fare. In late autumn if the soil is wet and heavy, apply lime or basic slag, about 4–8 ounces and 4 ounces respectively to the square yard, and less on neutral soils. Avoid plants intolerant of lime, like lupins, dieramas, astilbes, *Gentiana sino-ornata*, and epimediums, but place an extra quantity of ground chalk around dianthus, scabious, and pulsatillas. Prick over the surface where it has been trodden and make sure that the surface is level.

Winter in the herbaceous garden is a quiet time. Early on, root crowns of plants that are winter-tender or that break into growth very early should be given extra protection of litter, twigs, dry bracken, dry leaves, ashes, or sand. Eremuri, roscoeas, agapanthus, *Alstroemeria* Ligtu Hybrids, *Lilium regale*, *L. auratum*, and *Gunnera manicata* are benefited by such treatment. Coarse sand, grit, or coal ashes are useful around plants subject to attack by slugs, like delphiniums, incarvilleas, campanulas, and lupins. Plate 84 shows delphiniums after an application of coke ashes. Gunneras are best protected by pulling the old leaves over the crown or with a burlap sack. Rheums can be protected similarly. Paeonies should be mulched with old manure or compost, this serving the dual purpose of feeding the roots and protecting in very cold weather the fat red growth buds which are perilously near the surface. After a frost followed by a thaw, plants tend to work out of the ground, especially in newly planted borders. Keep watch, and firm by treading all plants that show heaving tendencies (Plate 85). In February sow seeds and take cuttings of stooled plants like dahlias, delphiniums, blue salvias, etc. (see p. 104).

84. Covering delphiniums in late autumn with coke ashes as a
protection against slugs.

85. Firming clumps of hemerocallis by treading after winter frosts.
A board is extended over the wet sticky soil.

86. A corner of a border after pricking over in early spring.

Spring ushers in the busiest season of all. Don't be too impatient, however, for it is a great mistake to work a border before the frost is thoroughly out of the ground or while the soil is wet and heavy. What is accomplished will not outweigh the harm. When the ground is workable remove litter and mulches, clean up the border, firm all plants, prick over or dig between plants (Plate 86, 87), incorporating dressings of manure, and lifting and dividing clumps as necessary. Now cope with plants like *Aster amellus*, erigerons (Plate 88), pyrethrums, all grey-foliaged plants, cultivars of *Chrysanthemum maximum* like 'Esther Read' and 'Wirral Pride', and *Penstemon heterophyllus*, transplanting and dividing them. Set out new plants that may have arrived from the nursery and move in other plants from the reserve beds, making sure that groupings are in accordance with last year's notes or new plans made in the course of the winter. Feed special clumps as required – ground chalk or mortar rubble for dianthuses and scabious, bone meal on neutral and acid soils as a general tonic, sieved compost on clumps of plants like heucheras, irises, and Michaelmas daisies which have risen out of the ground, making sure to firm them by treading first. A top-dressing of chopped, well-rotted manure or garden compost may be worked into the

87. A border showing early spring growth. Note groupings of plants.

88. *Erigeron* 'Festivity', a plant for spring planting like pyrethrums.

top few inches of the soil, or if this is not available a light dressing of a balanced commercial fertilizer is beneficial. In spring phosphates are particularly needed to stimulate root growth, just as nitrates will assure healthy dark-green foliage. Both of these are provided for in general-purpose fertilizers, which can be scattered on the surface or first mixed with granulated peat. Applications should not exceed 4 to 5 ounces to the square yard, but the manufacturer's directions should be studied, as some are stronger than others. There are in addition special fertilizers or foods prepared for special genera like irises, dahlias, and chrysanthemums.

In late spring, when danger of frost is largely over, cuttings prepared from pentstemons, lobelias, delphiniums, and chrysanthemums can be moved to their permanent homes. Water the border if there is a long, dry period, and pay particular attention to newly divided plants. Bulbous subjects like *Galtonia candicans* and new montbretias, or crocosmias as they are now called, should be set out. These late-flowering bulbous subjects are excellent in the border, as they do not leave gaps as do bulbs like tulips, narcissi, and hyacinths.

The staking of plants must start in late April or May, as poppies, anchusas, and thalictrums will be well up and must have support before their stems kink or blow down. As pointed out in Chapter 6, early staking of the whole border is important.

As far as pests and diseases are concerned, spring problems are minor, the worst enemies being slugs, and snails too when weather is warmer. The former function all winter and go to work in early spring, particularly attacking the tender, succulent new shoots of delphiniums, lupins, *Dicentra spectabilis* (Plate 89), and hostas. Sharp sand, grit, or coke ashes are deterrents, and poisoned meal (see p. 129) is a possible control. Paeonies if previously affected by Blotch or Botrytis should be sprayed with Bordeaux Mixture (see p. 193). Caterpillars, woodlice, and leather jackets can be trapped with poisoned baits made with Paris Green and bran. Aphis and capsid bugs, which are much worse in some seasons than others, are best controlled with sprays of Malathion, BHC, derris, and pyrethrum (see p. 131). Other than these there are few serious pests or diseases in the border in spring.

Summer in the border is a busy season but certainly the

89. *Dicentra spectabilis*, beloved by slugs.

90. An early border with *Paeonia officinalis*, lupins, and day lilies.

pleasantest, as most herbaceous borders are at their best. We not only work but enjoy the results of previous efforts. It is also the time to be critical and to analyse defects in the colour scheme, groupings, and heights. The notebook should be constantly in use. In early summer complete the last of the staking, making sure that all supports are in position in plenty of time to ensure natural effects. Pinch out the growing tips of plants like artemisias, heleniums, salvias, etc., to encourage a bushy branching habit (see p. 92).

Plants which need a little extra nourishment can be given a liberal dose of liquid manure, as outlined on p. 78, or fed with a sprinkling of dried blood. As heavy feeders, like dahlias, respond to a fertilizer with a high nitrogen content, a light dusting with nitrate of chalk or sulphate of ammonia is recommended, but only *if*, the 'if' being that it is applied sparingly on a still day so that none blows on to the foliage, that it is worked into the surface of the soil with a hoe or hand cultivator, and lastly that the area is well watered to remove any particles that have landed on the leaves and to settle the dry fertiliser into the ground.

Watering in summer may become a problem, but, as explained in Chapter 5, when it is resorted to, then it must be thoroughly

91. *Artemisia palmeri,*
which has not been
pinched back as in
Plate 59.

and carefully done. The value of thoroughness cannot be over-emphasized.

One of the time-consuming occupations in summer is dead-heading. There is much joking about this refined task, usually the work of the distaff side of the household. Its objects are several – to keep the border and plants in a tidy condition, to encourage new growth and further flowers, and to strengthen the plants for another year. The removal of dead flowers is in itself a rewarding form of house-maiding to be encouraged. Evening primroses look grim the day after, as do soggy irises and the twisted blooms of hollyhocks.

I long ago learned not to entrust this exacting task to patient friends whose enthusiasm far outstrips their gardening knowledge. One lady in a burst of enthusiasm removed not only all the dead-heads, but became so enthralled in the process that she removed all the flowers and even some of the buds just showing colour as well, on the theory that these would be dead-heads by the time her hosts returned the next week-end from London, but forgetting that in the meantime the garden was to be open for charity.

Dead-heading is an art, and for the best results knowledge is

92. *Lilium regale* in the July border with heleniums to carry on.

needed of the individual habits of plants, as well as a realization of the general principle that if flowers are left to form seed this process exhausts the plant still more and at the same time draws further goodness from the soil. Surely the border already has enough to do with producing such a concentrated show of luxuriant foliage and flowers in a few months. Some seeds, of course, are decorative and may be left. The brilliant carmine seeds of *Paeonia* species, the amusing ruddy seed pods of *Dictamnus albus*, and the fuzzy heads of pulsatilla and *Anemone japonica* are part of the fun. Some plants, too, reproduce themselves successfully by seeds, and a few heads of these like astrantias, valerians, and campanulas should be left if required for further stock. For the rest, wise and timely treatment is advised.

With some plants the dead flowers are removed, taking the seed pods with them, with others the flower stalk is cut to the ground, as in the case of day lilies, agapanthuses, and anthericums, and with still others the flower-head is cut with a little stem but the bulk of the plant is left, for the leaves are the factories which build up strength and food in the form of chlorophyll. Delphiniums if cut to the ground will usually produce a second flower,

93. A July border with delphiniums, lupins, and geraniums.

but this is much smaller, and meanwhile there are large gaps in the border. As an alternative, the central flower spike is removed first to encourage lateral flowering shoots. When these have finished blooming, cut back the stalk to where there are good leaves, and train surrounding plants to cover the 2 to 4-foot stems remaining. Pea sticks and supports must be removed as clumps are cut down. *Salvia superba*, lupins, and verbascums may be treated similarly to induce further bloom on side shoots. Phloxes will often send out further flowering heads from the leaf axils. Granted that this second flush of bloom is less spectacular, it is always welcome with phloxes for the scent alone. *Lychnis chalcedonica*, cut back a few inches below the head, will send out new flowers on short laterals but in smaller clusters. Yes, dead-heading is an art. With experience and daring experimentation remarkable effects and achievements can be hoped for.

As mentioned in the previous chapter, certain plants respond to dividing after flowering. Irises are the classic example. If dealt with immediately the flowers are finished, divisions will bloom the following year. Instructions for dividing and replanting will be found on p. 184. Pyrethrums can also be divided after flower-

94. A mid-summer border with large-scale groupings.

95. A late border with Michaelmas daisies.

ing. In late August take cuttings of penstemons, fuchsias, geraniums, and other tender herbaceous plants to ensure a stock for the next season. Cuttings from the yellow anthemis and nepetas can be taken from new growths produced after cutting back the plants after flowering.

Summer is the time to make copious notes in your garden book. It is the time to sit and enjoy the beauty of the border and drink in its fragrance as the evening dew releases the scents of evening primroses, phloxes, pinks, and, as I am not a purist, patches of mignonette, white tobacco, and the insignificant night-scented stock, which can be tucked among the clumps. It is a time to enjoy the humming bird that sips the nectar from the long spurs of the columbine and the clouds of butterflies and moths that hover over the flat heads of the carmine flowers of *Sedum spectabile* and the pale gold of evening primroses. Enjoyment is one of the corollaries to the summer border.

9 · Pests and Diseases of Herbaceous Plants

Fortunately herbaceous plants if well grown are relatively free from insect pests and diseases. To be well grown is half the battle, as plants that are properly fed, watered, and cultivated should be much more resistant than plants that are undernourished or required to grow in airless, dank conditions foreign to their nature. In this respect plants are very like humans. Neither are benefited by too much pampering, yet both require certain basic environmental conditions.

Some seasons are very much worse than others. Excessive rains may cause waterlogged conditions on heavy soil, and plants will suffer accordingly, becoming unhealthy and even rotting, plants requiring good drainage and sunshine being the first to show the evil effects. Similarly in long dry spells plants tend to shrivel, their lower leaves turning yellow and dropping and the flowers becoming wizened and blasted. We have all seen phlox, which likes rich soil and moisture, withered and yellow, and delphiniums that have only reached a half of their usual stature. If watering is possible, a thorough soaking followed by a mulch to retain the moisture after breaking up the surface of the soil will prevent further damage.

Following rains, damp humid weather will encourage mildews, black spot, and other fungus diseases. Dry weather seems to benefit aphides one year, and wet weather is said to be the cause of a very severe plague the next one. So the gardener is subjected to vagaries of weather. He can, however, do much by protective measures rather than waiting for the trouble to appear in full spate. Prevention is more important than cure.

There are today many excellent insecticides and fungicides in liquid and powder form on the market. These appear under a variety of trade names, and most of them prepared by reliable houses are suitable, the basic poisons and remedies being the same. Follow manufacturers' directions implicitly and do not increase proportions by whim because the aphides or cockchafers are particularly voracious. Damage or even death to plants may result.

For full effectiveness, choose the best times for application. For example, DDT, derris dust, and sulphur powders are best applied on a still day after a heavy dew which will cause the particles to adhere to the leaves. Liquid sprays should be applied when the foliage is dry and there is no chance of immediate rain to wash it away before it has been effective. Sprays should not be applied during bright sunlight, as the leaves will show signs of sun scorch. Evening is the best time. Nicotine preparations are most efficacious at temperatures of 65° F. or higher.

The equipment required is limited – a blower for dust or even a piece of fine muslin will serve, a syringe with a fine nozzle, a small hand sprayer, or a knapsack sprayer which comes in a variety of different styles and sizes for individual requirements. Prices of the latter may seem high, but they have to be made of non-corrosive metals like brass or bronze and well made to ensure adequate pressures. A good sprayer is a wise investment, but only if properly cared for. Sprays, especially those containing copper compounds, should be mixed in wooden or enamelled receptacles, not galvanized metal. A special measuring spoon as well as a fine strainer should be designated for this purpose and no other. All liquids mixed from solids should be carefully strained through fine muslin to prevent clogging of the nozzle. Immediately after use sprayers should be thoroughly washed out and left upside down to drain.

When spraying remember that every part of the plant must be reached if it is to be fully efficacious. The undersides of the leaves as well as the upper surfaces, the stems, and flower buds must be drenched with a fine spray. A spreader will assure further distribution of the tiny droplets. Insecticides are of two kinds, Contact Washes and Internal Poisons. Contact Washes are particularly useful against insects with sucking mouth parts, like capsids, aphides (greenfly), scale insects, mealy bugs, and thrips. Internal Poisons are designed for pests like sawfly, larvae, chafers, and leaf-eating caterpillars.

A third class of insecticides must be mentioned. These are baits designed for woodlice, snails, slugs, cutworms, and leather jackets. Most of these are made with bran as a base and metaldehyde, Paris Green, and other deadly poisons, alas, dangerous to humans, birds, and animals as well as bugs and caterpillars for whom they are intended. Every possible precaution should be taken. Bait may be covered with wire netting to keep away dogs, cats, and birds.

With these very general remarks let us turn to the more prevalent pests so that they can first be identified and secondly controlled. In Chapter 12 the various enemies of chrysanthemums, dahlias, paeonies, delphiniums, irises, lupins, and Michaelmas daisies are considered under their respective heads.

Remedies should be repeated as directed so that the plants do not become reinfected, as often the spores or larvae may lie dormant or incubating in the soil ready to develop at a later date. Only by repeated application is a complete check or cure assured.

Badly infected plants must be drastically treated, especially if the trouble is a virulent one. Infected parts should be removed and burnt. If the whole plant seems to be diseased or the trouble originates below ground, remove the entire plant and treat the soil with a disinfectant such as Cheshunt Compound or the recognized spray for the disease, such as Bordeaux Mixture for Black Blotch where delphiniums have previously been planted. Burn diseased leaves and plants; never put them on the compost heap. If possible do not plant the same genus in the same area. If the ground has proved conducive to rhizome rot in irises, plant them elsewhere on well-drained soil and very shallow so that the sun can reach the top of the rhizomes. If phloxes have been infected with the dreaded eelworm, burn them and plant new stock from a reliable source in fresh ground.

Pests

Aphides are perhaps the most prevalent in the herbaceous border. These are what are known in common parlance as greenfly and blackfly, their prevalence occurring in that order. Greenfly is a misnomer, as they are often delicate shades of pink, brown, and mauve. They are sucking insects, puncturing the leaf or veins with sharp mouth parts and sucking out the sap. Young growing shoots are particularly succulent, and can soon be destroyed. Certain types excrete honeydew, on which ants feed, and it induces sooty moulds. Ladybirds feed on aphides (as do birds like tits) and help control these pests. The most effective controls are sprays of Malathion, nicotine-soap, BHC, and DDT emulsions. Derris and Pyrethrum are also quite efficacious. Every part of the plant must be covered, so the spray must be fine and under high pressure. Aphides attack a variety of herbaceous plants, including campanulas, poppies, aquilegias, dahlias, *Chrysanthemum maximum*, and dozens of others.

CAPSID BUGS attack chrysanthemums and dahlias and various other perennials. They are variously known as Tarnished Plant Bug and Bishop's Bug. These breed on weeds like groundsel, docks, and sorrel. They are greenish yellow insects, often mottled with reddish-brown. They are particularly active in August and September and are best controlled with emulsion sprays of DDT, BHC, nicotine-soap, or with a dusting of nicotine, but as they are sucking insects, any of the recognized contact controls are effective.

CATERPILLARS and CUTWORMS should be dealt with by insecticides such as DDT intended for internal poisoning, as they are leaf and stem consumers; or they may be collected manually.

EARWIGS are the particular enemy of chrysanthemums, dahlias, helianthus, and many other annual and herbaceous plants (Plate 96). They are nocturnal, hiding by day in curled-up leaves, hollow stems, refuse, bamboo canes, and any other likely hideout. The best control is to remove the possible hide-outs or to dust them with DDT and to try to trap them in canes, flower-pots filled with straw, etc. Plants that are being attacked should be sprayed or dusted with DDT.

EELWORMS are the most serious of all pests and the most difficult with which to cope. They are particularly apt to attack phloxes, chrysanthemums, and even some primulas and oenotheras. To make matters more difficult, they are invisible to the

96. An earwig easily identified by its rear pincers.

97. The typical frothy exudation of the Frog Hopper, also known as Cuckoo Spit.

naked eye, although their ravages are very apparent. Leaves turn yellow, then wither, become distorted, and die, and gradually stems are affected. There is no cure save the careful rooting out and burning of plants suspected of harbouring this accursed pest. If infection is suspected, stools of chrysanthemums and phloxes for propagation must be subjected to the hot-water treatment, but this is hardly a procedure for the amateur, though widely used by commercial growers.

FROG-HOPPERS or CUCKOO-SPIT as they are known when in the larval state, attack lavenders, roses, dianthus, and many other herbaceous plants, including many of the common weeds. They are most easily recognized by the white frothy foam (Plate 97) with which the yellowish-green larvae surround themselves when feeding. They can be controlled by a nicotine spray, but to be effective the foam must first be syringed off with water so that the spray reaches the larvae. Chrysanthemums are often affected in late August or September. Frog-hoppers breed in common weeds, so a war should be waged in the adjoining hedgerows and waste lands as well as in the border.

LEAF-MINERS are larvae of insects which do considerable damage by feeding on the tissue between the two skins of the leaf, destroying the powers of the leaf to assimilate and breathe. Plants attacked include chrysanthemums (Plate 98), irises, and various compositae. For control spray with BHC to destroy the parent insect and hand-pick and burn infected leaves.

MILLEPEDES (Plate 99). Black millepedes are often confused with centipedes, which are distinguished by their flat, brown bodies and their fewer pairs of legs and longer antennae. Millepedes are sluggish and usually coil themselves up when disturbed. They are hard and shell-like. Unlike centipedes, which are beneficial, they do some damage, but it is of a secondary nature, following the work of slugs or woodlice. They feed on decaying matter, and hence sometimes attack rotting lily bulbs or dahlia tubers. They may be controlled by trapping with potatoes, beetroots, or turnips which have been hollowed out and buried

98. A chrysanthemum leaf showing marked injury by Leaf-Miners.

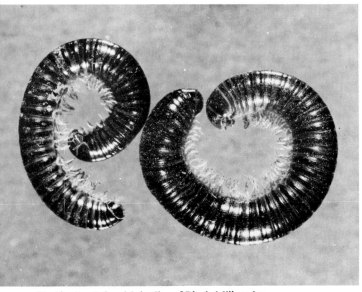

99. The hard sluggish bodies of Black Millepedes.

beneath the soil. Lift these every two days. Frequent cultivation disturbs them, and a liberal application of lime in winter or a dusting with DDT or Aldrin is effective.

SLUGS and SNAILS are best trapped with poison bait incorporating metaldehyde, but they too may be collected and destroyed (see p. 129). As they are active at night, a search with a torch is almost always rewarding if they are prevalent. A metaldehyde spray is also effective in fine weather.

WIREWORMS are prevalent on poor soil and in gardens recently formed from pasture land or fields. Wireworms are long and thin, pale brown, and six-legged (Plate 102). They live on the old roots of turf, but in gardens turn their attentions to the roots of other plants. They may be controlled by trapping. Bury potatoes or carrots on wooden skewers in infested soils. Lift these daily and destroy the wireworms. Cultivate carefully, destroying all weeds. Dusts like Aldrin and BHC are effective controls when worked into the top few inches of soil, and will also destroy Swift moth caterpillars, leatherjackets, and chafer grubs. Persistence and good cultivation will in time free the soil.

WOODLICE are troublesome, particularly in old gardens where there are borders with wooden edges or where there are piles of old timbers, rotting garden refuse, plant boxes, or packing. They are easily identifiable by their seven pairs of legs and oval, segmented, and flattened body. Like snails and slugs, they are nocturnal, hiding by day under piles of rubbish, between paving-stones, under crates, or in any other equally dark, moist spot. Woodlice live on decayed matter, but they also eat foliage and the roots in the bottom of flower-pots. Trap them by much the same methods as used for earwigs, or poison them with bait made from 1 ounce of Paris Green mixed with a pound of bran and a little water. Spread this bait over the areas where control is desired at roughly the rate of 1 ounce per square yard. Equally effective is a similar bait in which 2 lb. of dried blood is substituted for 1 lb. of bran. If possible, hiding-places should be removed. Where this is not practical these should be sprayed or dusted with DDT.

135

100. An adult Slug and the injury it causes.

101. The eggs of the Field Slug on the dark surface of the soil.

102. The larvae of the serious pest Wireworms.

Diseases

BOTRYTIS. This is a common fungus disease, especially in wet seasons. Lilies are particularly susceptible, and paeonies to a milder degree. It may be detected by water-soaked circular patches on the leaves which subsequently turn grey or white, with a greyish mould on the leaf surfaces. Madonna lilies and regales are both susceptible. At the first signs of this disease spray with Bordeaux Mixture.

LEAFY-GALL is caused by a fungus disease which attacks carnations, chrysanthemums, verbascums, hollyhocks, sweet williams, etc. It is identified by a gall-like growth with a mass of crowded, short, leafy shoots, not unlike a cauliflower. Destroy infected plants and propagate from clean stock.

MILDEW is caused by a fungus. There are two types, Powdery and Downy. The former, which is more superficial, attacks Michaelmas daisies, delphiniums, limoniums, and chrysanthemums (Plate 103) particularly. It can be controlled by spraying or dusting at weekly or bi-weekly intervals with Bordeaux Mixture or copper lime dust. Remove and burn badly infected leaves or growths. Powdery Mildew is easily identifiable by white mould on the leaf surfaces. Downy Mildew is more deep-seated, and is first noticed by yellowing patches on the leaves and the presence of a whitish or bluish grey mealy growth on the undersides. Plants so infected should be removed, and the healthy plants sprayed or dusted as for Powdery Mildew. Mildew is more prevalent in wet seasons and in overcrowded, airless gardens.

MOSAIC of lilies is indicated by streaking and discoloration of the foliage. Leaves may be streaked with yellow or mottled with dark- and light-green blotches. Gradually plants become stunted and deformed. They should be rogued out and destroyed in order to preserve clean stock. Lilies grown from seed are virus-free, and hence the value of this form of propagation.

RUST attacks a variety of plants, particularly hollyhocks (*Althaea rosea*), the closely related tree mallows (*Lavatera olbia*), and

103. Chrysanthemum foliage attacked by mildew.

the musk mallow (*Malva moschata*). Rust is a fungus which attacks the leaves and stems, particularly of plants suffering from drought or lack of nourishment. Brownish-black pustules appear on the undersides of the leaves, which become badly discoloured and wither. There is no effective control. Infected leaves should be burnt and new stocks of seedlings raised to replace existing stocks frequently. Hollyhocks, in fact, are often treated as biennials.

SOOTY MOULD is a secondary disease resulting from aphides or scale insects. It is readily identified by the black, dirty layer on the leaf surface. It can be removed with a sponge, but the cure is to destroy the pest which is attacking the plant and exuding sticky excretions which act as a culture for the mould.

WILT is a common disease of asters, particularly of Michaelmas daisies (*Aster novi-belgii*) and *A. novae-angliae*. The lower leaves wither, starting from the ground. The fungus lives in the root-stocks and secretes a fluid which causes the lower leaves to wither, starting from the ground. Destroy badly infected plants. Use sterilized soil when possible and try to select varieties known to be wilt-resistant.

104. A fine example of a mixed border with shrubs
and herbaceous plants.

10 · The Mixed Border

There is no doubt that because of modern labour difficulties the mixed border is today as popular as the true herbaceous border, if not more so. By 'mixed border' we mean one in which hardy herbaceous plants are combined with shrub roses, flowering shrubs, and even spring bulbs and annuals (Plates 104, 105). In other words, one flower border may take the place of several or more specialized ones. This is ideal for small gardens. Furthermore, a mixed border is lovely in itself, with its bold masses of colour and the great variety of forms and foliage contrasts. It is possible to design borders which are looser and freer, with the undulating masses of roses and shrubs as well as herbaceous plants.

Another distinct advantage is the fact that a mixed border is partially clothed with plants throughout the winter and early spring, when the classic herbaceous border is a flat, bare expanse. Where gardens or borders are in close view of the house it is surely pleasanter to have interest the twelve months round. Shrubs with attractive fruits, the hips of roses, the evergreen leaves of a wide variety of suitable shrubs, the winter flowers of others, like *Viburnum fragrans*, *Chimonanthus praecox*, and *Mahonia japonica*, and the early comers that announce the advent of spring, like flowering currant, forsythia, and flowering quince, provide winter interest. Even the bare stems of many shrubs, like the Japanese bitter orange (*Aegle sepiaria*) with its brilliant green thorny twigs or the interesting layered habit of *Viburnum tomentosum* 'Mariesii', have fascination and charm.

A border can be predominantly shrubby, with clumps of suitable herbaceous plants grouped along the front and used as under-planting (Plate 105). It can be predominantly herbaceous, with flowering and foliage shrubs used singly or in groups to provide form and colour (Plate 106). For example, groups of lavenders, santolinas, shrubby potentillas, and dwarf berberises, such as *Berberis thunbergii atropurpurea nana* or *B. candidula*, used

105 A grey and blue shrub border with occasional clumps of herbaceous plants such as pinks, globe thistles, and hostas.

106. A mixed border in spring showing the groupings of shrubs at the back and spaces left at the front for annuals.

at the front of borders or worked into flower-beds are extremely effective throughout the year. Again, shrub roses carried well forward in a border or used in the middle distance give form and mystery, as they block the view so that the long sweep of the border is not visible at a glance. The point to remember is that the greater the quantity of shrubs, the more labour-saving the border becomes after it is once established.

Mixed borders have other advantages. The solid masses of shrubs introduced among the perennials help to give them support and to shield them from wind. This lightens the task of staking and tying. In shady borders shrubs are particularly useful, as there are excellent ones, like mahonias, hydrangeas, skimmias, fatsias, some rhododendrons, and pierises, which have great charm and combine well with herbaceous plants.

Planning the Mixed Border

It is important to decide at the outset the relative proportions of herbaceous and shrubby plants to be used. This will be dictated by the effect desired and the amount of time that you or others will be able to devote to the border. Where the area is large it is possible to plant broad masses of shrubs that will cover a considerable part of it, but the shrubs must be carefully selected for their habit and their foliage. In smaller borders shrubs must be scaled down so that there is a pleasing relationship between them and the masses of perennials. Although shrubs are usually reserved for the back of the border where height is required, do not hesitate to mass low-growing ones along the front as well. Too often borders are soft and rather bitty, with clumps of heucheras, nepetas, pinks, thrifts, and similar flowers at the front. They need the boldness not only of the sword-like leaves of irises, the heart-shaped foliage of hostas, and the strong heavy-textured rounded leaves of bergenias but also of the solid masses of shrubs like lavenders, santolinas, rugosa roses, box wood, evergreen berberis, rosemary, and caryopteris.

In selecting shrubs consider their habits carefully. To cut down labour choose those that cover the ground so that weeds are blanketed. For example, *Senecio laxifolius* (Plate 107) is indispensable, as it sprawls on the ground in a mound of silvery grey.

143

107. *Senecio laxifolius*, one of the best of grey foliage shrubs.

Similarly, the two varieties of *Viburnum tomentosum* 'Mariesii' and 'Lanarth' are superb in large mixed borders, as each blankets as much as 8 to 10 feet with its spreading almost horizontal branches and provides a spectacular display of white flowers in May. In small borders where space is precious the choice of shrubs must be dictated by two criteria. They must either be small and compact in habit, occupying little ground space, or erect like a standard rose, lilac, or broom so that there is space for herbaceous plants beneath them.

In planning select carefully, so that the shrubs, roses, and perennials enhance each other. Use the first two as a setting for the harmonizing or contrasting colours of the flowers and foliage of the herbaceous plants, so many of which have rather nondescript leaves in varying shades of green. Select shrubs with contrasting foliage in the grey, silver, golden, blue, and purple range. These are so decorative that their flowers are secondary. I remember hearing a friend ask 'What is that lovely patch of purplish-red flowers next to the silvery grey foliage?' What she was looking at across the lawn was a billowing mass of the purple-leaved rhus (*Rhus cotinus foliis purpureis* 'Notcutt's var.') partially concealed by a large clump of *Artemisia* 'Silver Queen'. As this chance remark proves, coloured foliage if cleverly used can be as effective as flowers themselves.

When designing a mixed border it is important to concentrate on the groupings. Get away from the idea of the perfectly arranged herbaceous border, with plants sloping from back to front with considerable uniformity. The shrubs at the back will, of course, be partly concealed as the plants grow up in front. Other shrubs carried well forward should have low underplantings so that they stand out boldly. Such herbaceous plants as *Geranium ibericum*, *G. endressii*, *Stachys lanata*, London pride, violas, dwarf erigeron, and heucheras are effectively used in this way.

Shrubs tend to grow rapidly, so do not place deep-rooted herbaceous plants too close to them, as it may be necessary to transplant them the following year. Use plants that are easily moved and quick to establish. For example, do not plant alstroemerias, dictamnus, or paeonies in a position where they will soon be encroached upon by *Viburnum tomentosum* 'Mariesii', the robust roses 'Frühlingsgold' or 'Nevada' (Plate 108), or a large philadelphus. Instead choose *Lychnis coronaria*, anthemis, Michaelmas daisies, or foxgloves. Leave ample space between the groupings of shrubs and clumps of herbaceous plants, just as you leave more space between the clumps in a border than between the individual plants.

In spite of careful planning, the mixed border will need constant attention to keep it in order, and as shrub roses and flowering bushes develop there will have to be alterations in the

108. Rose 'Nevada' underplanted with irises.

herbaceous planting. Do not forget that the shrubs will increase in size out of all proportion to the clumps of herbaceous plants. The clumps will grow denser as the plants establish. Not so the ceanothus, weigela, or lilac, which will grow larger each year in spite of pruning. If shrubs are too heavily pruned they never develop their true natural habit and beauty.

Suggested Shrubs for Mixed Borders

It is impossible here to list more than a few of the most suitable shrubs for mixed borders. I have already mentioned grey foliage. The various varieties of lavender (Plate 9) are probably the most useful of all, ranging from the dwarf forms of *Lavandula spica*, such as *nana atropurpurea* and 'Folgate var.', to the larger *L.* 'Twickel Purple' and *L. vera*. Groups along the front of borders are most effective, and the flowers and foliage enhance any colour scheme, harmonizing alike with yellows, pinks, and reds. Santolinas are also excellent, but they must be cut back each spring to keep them compact in habit. *Senecio laxifolius* certainly provides the almost perfect grey foliage shrub. It is hardy, evergreen, and quick growing. It has a good spreading habit and can be cut back hard when it becomes leggy and thus controlled in size, so that a plant may occupy a circular area from 3 to 7 feet in diameter. *Elaeagnus macrophylla, angustifolia*, and *umbellata* are all attractive shrubs for the larger mixed border, as is sea buckthorn.

Red and purple foliage shrubs, besides the rhus and dwarf berberis already mentioned, include Japanese maples, purple-leaved sage (*Salvia officinalis purpurea*), and the elegant *Rosa rubrifolia*, which has delicate colouring in tones of mauve, silver, and purple. All these are particularly effective with white or pink flowers and with any silver-leaved plants, either shrubby or herbaceous, including artemisias, *Stachys lanata*, helichrysums, and *Lychnis coronaria*.

Useful flowering shrubs include forsythias, lilacs, abelias, kolkwitzias, weigelas, viburnums, and brooms. Outstanding are ceanothus and philadelphus. In summer the soft blue panicles of *Ceanothus* 'Gloire de Versailles' harmonize with many of the herbaceous-border plants like phloxes, sidalceas, and blue salvias, and there is such a wide range of philadelphus, both species and hybrids, that there is a plant for almost any scale border. *P. microphyllus* is a scented treasure for small borders or for massing in the front of larger ones. Then there are medium-sized growers like 'Manteau d'Hermine' *P. lemoinei erectus*, and 'Sybille'. For larger borders, 'Belle Étoile', 'Beauclerk', 'Enchantment', and *P. burfordiensis* are among the best. Their myriads of heavily perfumed flowers make them invaluable for border displays as well as for cutting.

The delicate glaucous foliage of rue is delightful in a border, associating beautifully with plants like yellow anthemis, sweet williams, campanulas, and shrubby· potentillas. The last are among the best of all shrubs for the mixed border. They range in height from plants like 'Katherine Dykes' and 'Farrer's White', which are 4 to 5 feet high, to dwarf forms like *P. nana argentea*

109. *Helianthemum* 'The Bride' with *Betonica grandiflora robusta*.

110. *Romneya coulteri* which combines well with shrubs and herbaceous plants.

and *mandschurica*. The latter are effective along the front of a border, especially where they can spill over the path or paved terrace, in association with nepeta, lavender, erigerons, and heucheras. Sun roses, particularly forms of *Helianthemum mummularium*, are invaluable in the mixed border used in a similar way (Plate 109). They flower profusely from mid-May until the end of June and come in a wonderful range of colours, including carmine, deep flame, orange, pink, ivory, gold, and canary yellow. They are delightful in association with herbaceous plants, as the possibilities of striking colour combinations are almost endless. Cistuses are useful for hot, sunny borders and will stand dry conditions.

The tree poppy, *Romneya coulteri*, or the hybrid *R. trichocalyx*, is a particularly effective shrub, with its huge, crinkled white flowers with brilliant gold centres and deeply cut glaucous foliage (Plate 110). It too likes a warm sunny position. Although sometimes slow to establish, it ramps where happy. It is best to cut it to the ground each spring like a herbaceous plant, although it may not be killed back in mild areas. Tree lupins are also happy in mixed borders, though not on chalk, as they are intolerant of lime. There is a lovely pure white called 'Snow Queen' and a deep yellow, 'Golden Spire'. They form spreading shrubs up to 5-feet tall. Old plants are apt to succumb in severe winters, and at best they are short-lived. Their scented flower spikes are effective with anchusas, pink and deep-red oriental poppies, irises, and delphiniums. They also combine happily with lavender, potentillas, and rosemary (Plate 111).

Plate 112 shows another first-class plant for the mixed border, *Euphorbia wulfenii*. It must be placed so that its full beauty can be enjoyed, as it forms a low, mounded mass and should not be buried in a mass of leafy herbage. *Phlomis fruticosa* (Plate 113) is equally attractive, both for its felted leaves and its whorls of yellow hooded flowers. It is peculiarly suited to combination with herbaceous plants, and should enjoy greater popularity than it does. Hardy fuchsias and hypericums are also delightful in the mixed border.

Old-fashioned roses (Plate 114), floribundas, hybrid perpetuals, and rose species can be satisfactorily combined with herbaceous

149

111. *Rosmarinus officinalis*, an indispensable aromatic shrub.

112. *Euphorbia wulfenii*, a first-class shrub with glaucous foliage and a spreading habit.

150

113. The sun-loving *Phlomis fruticosa* backed by delphiniums.

114. A border of old roses and irises, with acanthus and lavender on the left.

115. *Paeonia* 'Souvenir de Maxime Cornu'.

plants. Be careful of some of the former, as their flowering period is very short and the mass of subsequent foliage is often nondescript and in certain areas subject to mildew and black spot. Some of the perpetual-flowering modern floribundas, like 'Magenta', 'Rosemary Rose', and 'Geranium Red', have very full, flat flowers similar to some of the old Bourbons and Centifolias. Rugosa types, with their heavily scented flowers freely borne, colourful hips in winter, bold, wrinkled, clear-green foliage, and their sturdy mounded habit make good border plants. Hybrid Musks are again a good choice, although their flowering season is limited to early summer and autumn. Roses are charming when underplanted with *Viola cornuta, Geranium endressii, G. sanguineum lancastriense,* dwarf campanulas, London Pride, or old-fashioned single pinks and associated with clumps of lilies, irises, delphiniums, and paeonies (Plate 115).

Yuccas are magnificent bold plants for the mixed border, with their spectacular, spiky, evergreen foliage and huge candelabras of creamy white flowers (Plate 116).

In summary, use shrubs and herbaceous plants to enhance each other. Exclude plants not suitable and try to make the most of the form, habit, texture, colour, and even fragrance of both flowers and foliage. It is far more difficult to design an effective mixed border than an herbaceous one. But because of the longer season of interest of the former, its practicality to modern conditions, and its great charm it is worth the extra effort. Lastly, the mixed border offers an excellent opportunity to use large rather architectural herbaceous plants like *Aruncus sylvester* (Plate 117), *Acanthus mollis, Rheum palmatum, Heracleum mantegazzianum* (giant parsnip), and ornamental grasses like *Arundo donax* and *Cortaderia argentea* (Pampas grass).

116. Yuccas with their bold spikey foliage and pyramids of ivory
     white blooms.

117. *Aruncus sylvester*, a massive herbaceous plant for shrubberies.

118. *Lilium candidum*, an excellent lily for late June borders.

119. *Lilium* 'Enchantment' is an easy lily for borders or shrubberies.

120. *Meconopsis betonicifolia.*

11 · Herbaceous Plants for Woodland Gardens

In addition to their use in borders, beds, and conventional garden schemes, herbaceous plants are extremely useful for the natural wild or woodland gardens which have become so popular since the War as a result of their labour-saving nature. Herbaceous plants also play an important role in water or bog gardens, which are often included in the above. Obviously plants selected for such divergent uses must be varied in their habits and their requirements, but many of those mentioned in this chapter are equally suited to a border.

Woodland gardens rely almost entirely for their effectiveness upon three groups of plants – trees, shrubs, and hardy herbaceous plants, the last chosen for both their flowers and their foliage. Owing to the canopy of trees there is inevitably shade, and the heavier this is, the more restricted is the range of possible perennials, most of which enjoy or tolerate semi-shade or dappled shade but not dark, overhanging canopies of foliage. Soil conditions of course vary, but there is often rich humus and leaf mould. Moisture is important, for many plants like both semi-shade and a cool, moist root run. This is particularly true of the spectacular blue Himalayan poppies (Plate 120), including *Meconopsis betonicifolia*, *grandis*, and *simplicifolia*, candelabra primulas (Plate 121), and lilies such as 'Maxwill' (Plate 122), martagons, and American *Lilium canadense*, *superbum* (Plate 123), and Bellingham Hybrids.

Preparation of planting sites should be thorough. Leaf mould, well-rotted compost, and horticultural peat should be worked in where the soil is deficient in humus or in moisture-retention properties. Be sure drainage is good and that the young plants have air even if in shade. In woodland gardens there is a tendency for plants to be crowded and subsequently to be overgrown by taller shrubs. Proper spacing will pay dividends in future, as the best effects are usually the result of established groups or colonies

159

121. The Bartley Strain of *Primula pulverulenta* with *P. japonica* in a cool moist position.

which have naturalized. To avoid spotty planting allow groups to trail off among the trees, with here and there an odd plant placed apart from the group.

Spring Flowers

Some of the most attractive herbaceous plants for the wild garden make a very early appearance. Primroses and polyanthuses are as much a part of spring as daffodils, and they are of easy cultivation. Polyanthus can be grown from seed sown in pans or boxes in June or as soon as the seeds of last year's crop are ripe. The seedlings, grown on in boxes or frames in a cool, moist position, should be planted out in their permanent homes, where they will flower the following spring. Special favourites must be

122. *Lilium* 'Maxwill', excellent for light shaded positions.

123. The North American *Lilium superbum* forming a vigorous clump.

124. The nodding heads of *Helleborus orientalis*.

treated as clones and propagated by division after flowering. Primroses, both single and double, should be treated in the same way. When planting polyanthuses in woodland avoid the look of bedding out. Nothing is less appropriate. Like primroses, they are particularly attractive when scattered among spring bulbs.

Hellebores are admirable in the wild garden, as they flower early and for a prolonged period, their foliage is beautiful, and they colonize happily. Most suitable are the lovely Lenten roses, *Helleborus orientalis*, and its many hybrids (Plate 124). These flower from February to April and come in lovely colours ranging from greenish pink and cream to deep rose and purple. The nodding, beautifully formed flowers unfortunately do not keep well in water but boiling briefly the tips of the stems immediately after cutting helps. Hellebores need adequate moisture throughout the summer and should be mulched if planted in dry positions. They

125. The very long-lasting *Helleborus corsicus*.

are tolerant of lime; in fact, some of the best in this country grow in a famous chalk garden. They resent disturbance, moving best when still seedlings; larger plants should be lifted just after flowering. Of the green-flowered species *H. corsicus* (Plate 125), with its handsome toothed, bluish-green leaves, and the dark evergreen *H. foetidus* and *H. viridis* are outstanding.

The early yellow daisy-like leopard's bane *Doronicum planta-gineum* is a charming plant (Plate 126). It likes semi-shade and moisture. The varieties 'Harpur Crewe' and 'Miss Mason' both have bright-green foliage and are excellent for cutting, as the erect stems grow to a height of 2 to $2\frac{1}{2}$ feet before producing their large-rayed single flowers in April through May. Another particularly attractive plant is the American *Mertensia virginica*, with silvery green foliage and clusters of pendulous pink buds which open into tubular blue flowers (Plate 127). Moist soil, especially in spring, is essential. After flowering the stems die to the ground. Mertensia is best when left to spread and colonize through open glades and light shrubberies.

126. Early flowering doronicums, also known as Leopard's Bane.

127. *Mertensia virginica.*

Another early blue flower is *Brunnera macrophylla*, which resembles a rather tall forget-me-not, with coarse, heart-shaped, basal leaves and 18-inch stems bearing panicles of brilliant blue flowers. It will thrive in sun or light shade, and can be successfully divided in spring or early autumn. *Cynoglossum nervosum* is a similar plant with gentian-blue flowers appearing in July. Bugle (*Ajuga*), with its blue flowers and low-growing habit, makes a fine ground cover for the wild garden. Although it will spread rapidly, it is not particularly invasive. *A. reptans* and its var. *atropurpurea* with purple foliage are excellent. *A. genevensis* is more compact in habit and requires more sun. Another very useful low-growing plant is the lungwort, which flowers from late March well into May. *Pulmonaria angustifolia* sends up numerous 8-inch stems of pinkish flowers, which turn blue with age. There is a red species known as *rubra*. *P. saccharata* grows a little taller and has variegated leaves, marbled with white, and flowers which range from pink to red and violet. There is also the attractive Jacob's Ladder, *Polemonium caeruleum*, which produces its panicles of blue flowers throughout the summer and the dwarfer 'Blue Pearl'.

One of the most useful of all ground covers for dry, shady places is the St John's Wort, *Hypericum calycinum*, which forms a dense mass of roots and stems. This tends to be shrubby in nature, but can be cut to the ground early each spring to encourage a mass of bushy growth and myriads of saucer-shaped golden flowers.

Lily of the valley (*Convallaria majalis*) is another splendid ground cover for shady places, either under trees or in the shelter of a north wall. It requires a rich, leafy loam and does not like a dry position. Plant the roots so that the crowns are not more than an inch at most below the surface of the soil. Early autumn is the best time for lifting, dividing, and replanting. They are beautiful in early spring, when the brilliant emerald green of the unfurling green makes a carpet, soon to be scattered with heavily perfumed spikes of white lilies. The best variety is 'Fortin's Giant' which is well worth the extra cost.

The easily propagated London Pride (*Saxifraga umbrosa*) is

another useful carpeter. It is happy in sun or shade and will ramp in good moderately moist soil. The compact masses of neat green rosettes are lovely in themselves, and the panicles of tiny flowers like a haze of pink smoke are enchanting in a season which lasts from May to July. Bergenias (Plate 29), are good plants for light shade, and their bold leaves and arching panicles of pink to rosy purple flowers are useful for cutting in spring. Good species include *B. cordifolia* (Plate 128), with white, pink, and purple varieties, *purpurascens*, dwarf in habit but with very large individual flowers in June; the March-flowering but sometimes tender *stracheyi*, and lastly *crassifolia,* with large, fleshy leaves. *B. ligulata* is one of the earliest to flower, its large sprays of pink often opening in February. The foliage of most of these turns rich shades of purple, bronze, and crimson in winter.

Tiarella cordifolia, attractively known as the North American foam flower, has a dwarf creeping habit and masses of tiny feathery plumes of white flowers on 9-inch stems in May and June. *T. wherryi* is more compact and slightly taller. It flowers intermittently throughout the summer and early autumn. Both like cool, damp root runs in leafy or peaty soil. Divide them after they have flowered or in very early spring when the leaves are just appearing. The cross between *Tiarella* and *Heuchera* has produced the lovely recently introduced *Heucherella* 'Bridget Bloom', a very desirable perennial for sun or half shade with 18-inch panicles of delightful, little, pink, star-shaped flowers.

Other low-growing plants of great distinction are the members of the genus *Epimedium*. The delicate wiry-stemmed leaves, heart-shaped and often colouring rich bronze in autumn, would make these plants desirable even if the flowers were not so delicately attractive. The flowers in early spring, often appearing before the leaves, range in colour from white, pale yellow, and pink to purple and coppery orange. Species include *E. pinnatum* (yellow), *alpinum* (purple), *perralderianum* (yellow), and *grandiflorum*, colours here including white, pink, purple, and yellow. There are hybrids as well, like *E. warleyense* and *youngianum*, and named forms like 'Rose Queen'.

128. *Bergenia cordifolia.*

Fine Foliage

Probably pride of place for fine foliage for shady places must go to the plantain lily, known correctly as *Hosta* but more familiarly as *Funkia*. These superb Asiatic plants require rich, damp soil, shade or semi-shade, and protection from slugs and snails (see p. 135). Divide hostas in early spring when the fat new shoots are visible. Old clumps are best cut apart with a spade, as they are very solid and heavy. When possible leave clumps undisturbed so that they may grow to their full beauty (Plate 129). The largest-leaved species include *H. fortunei, ventricosa,* and *sieboldiana,* all with huge, glaucous, heart-shaped leaves and long spikes of lilac flowers. Other species, such as *H. undulata* and *H. lancifolia* var. *albo-marginata,* have variegated leaves. There are smaller plants as well, so consult your nurserymen's catalogues to find just the plant for which you are looking.

Solomon's Seal (*Polygonatum multiflorum*) is a beautiful foliage plant, tolerant of fairly heavy shade. It likes moist, leafy soil, and when established sends up gracefully arching stems, from which clusters of small green and creamy white flowers hang at the leaf axils. The fleshy horizontal root-stocks with fat growth buds should be planted in autumn several inches below the surface and they will gradually seek their own level. A plant, similar in habit but with showy terminal clusters of flowers, is the N. American *Smilacina racemosa,* which enjoys similar conditions (Plate 131).

Other American favourites for the woodland garden include the wood lilies (*Trillium*), characterized by the whorls of leaves in threes and petals and sepals in threes as well, thus explaining the name. Cool, moist, shady conditions and leaf mould are their delight. They flower in late April, May, and early June. The showy white *T. grandiflorum* (Plate 3), which turns to rose as it ages, and the large *T. nervosum* are among the most spectacular. The May apple or American mandrake *Podophyllum peltatum* and the closely allied Indian *P. emodi* are equally desirable plants for the wild garden.

A few other foliage plants merit attention. Rodgersias are magnificent dramatic plants for herbaceous or mixed borders and wild gardens. They like semi-shade and moist, peaty soil. Wind is their

129. *Hosta sieboldiana.*

130. The early flower-
ing *Fritillaria im-
perialis* 'Aurora',
equally suited to
an open glade
and the mixed
border.

171

131. *Smilacina racemosa*, a fragrant flower with elegant foliage.

enemy, so find a sheltered position, but give them space so that their superb decorative leaves and flower-heads can be appreciated (Plate 5). Their heavy rhizomes are easily divided in spring. *Rodgersia aesculifolia* thrives in very moist positions, its panicles of pale pink flowers contrast strikingly with the huge bronzed horse-chestnut leaves. Other species include *R. pinnata* with more pronouncedly cut leaves, *R. tabularis* and *podophylla*, all of which attain a height of 3 to 4 feet and flower in July. Equally effective is *Peltiphyllum peltatum*, once classed under *Saxifraga*. It is grown primarily for its bold circular leaves borne on 3- to 4-foot stems, which earn it the name umbrella plant (Plate 5). The flesh-pink flowers appear in early spring before the leaves develop. The root-stock of mature plants is a network of huge rhizomes which crawl about on the surface in damp positions. It needs rich, deep soil for the side roots. Old plants are true curiosities of great character. The round, smooth leaves are a wonderful foil for the rough compound leaves of rodgersias described above.

Ferns are almost perfect herbaceous plants for shady borders, shrubberies, town gardens, and difficult places where little else will grow. There are species for moist, shady positions and there are others for dry, shady ones or dry, sunny ones. Catalogues of fern specialists should be consulted for appropriate species.

Mostly for Flowers

Campanulas are useful plants for naturalizing. *C. lactiflora* thrives in light shade, the 5- to 6-foot stems of flowers making bold masses of pale colours, which are particularly effective with lilies like the Bellingham Hybrids, which flower simultaneously in late June and July. *C. latifolia* is another bold bell-flower, effective with plants like foxgloves, *Lilium giganteum*, and meconopsis in a woodland setting. Both these species take some time to establish, particularly the former. They can be grown from seed, from divisions, or from cuttings in spring if need be. The delightful *C. persicifolia* (Plate 33) can be used effectively in light shade, as can the showy purple *C. glomerata*, both of which spread rapidly and present no difficulties.

Foxgloves are delightful woodland plants, thriving and seeding themselves in the leaf mould. Initial stock can be raised from seed. Sow the seeds in April or early May in a box of carefully prepared seed compost and plant out the seedlings when they are large enough to handle. They will flower the following spring. From here on they will pretty much look after themselves, if the flower-heads are left until after the seeds have ripened and dispersed. Aconitums are tolerant of light shade and make a good effect when planted in fairly large masses. Other herbaceous plants tolerant of light shade but which must be used carefully for good effect in a woodland garden include phloxes, bleeding hearts (*Dicentra spectabilis*) (Plate 89), and meadow rues (*Thalictrum*) (Plate 27).

The geranium is a useful woodland plant. (I am not, of course, referring to the house plant or bedder which is really a pelargonium.) Geraniums lend themselves to naturalization in semishade or sun. They are easily propagated by division, and many

173

of them seed freely. For wild gardens *Geranium grandiflorum* is particularly desirable, with its greyish green, attractively cut foliage and abundant masses of flat, rich blue flowers with red veining borne on 18-inch stems. *G. ibericum* is similar but has a rather longer flowering season, extending through July into August, and the flowers are more violet in tone and perhaps a little taller. *G. endressii* is a valuable low-growing plant for the wild garden, with bright pink, veined-red, five-petalled flowers throughout the summer. 'Wargrave Var.' is an even pink and 'Russell Pritchard' is a deeper rose. *G. macrorrhizum* 'Ingwersen Var.' is an 18-inch plant with large woody roots, bright pink flowers, and faintly aromatic leaves. It enjoys semi-shade. Like *G. endressii*, it should be more widely planted. *G. phaeum*, called the mourning widow because of its sombre black-purple flowers, is tolerant of shade and is an interesting addition. *G. pratense*, the native meadow crane's bill, has 2- to 3-foot stems bearing an abundance of soft blue flowers from July to September. There is the old-fashioned double form known as *flore pleno*, a white form *album*, and the amusingly striped and veined *striatum*. Outstanding among other species is the spectacular *G. psilostemon* (*G. armenum*), with sensational flowers of vivid magenta-red with black centres, borne in profusion in May and June. This is not a favourite with everyone, but it is a very striking and useful plant.

Unusual Plants for Light Shade

The list grows, and there are still many fine plants worthy of mention. I shall merely list a few of my favourites. Although the purplish-lilac flowers are unspectacular, *Iris foetidissima* is a splendid plant. Its foliage is handsome throughout the year, and its brilliant orange fruits are a spot of colour in the depths of winter. Best of all, it succeeds under difficult conditions in heavy shade. The toad lily *Tricyrtis hirta* and *T. macropoda* are exotic curiosities which flower in late summer or early autumn. The flowers, white or greenish yellow liberally spotted with purple and borne in the axils of the leaves, are arresting. They grow from 2 to 3 feet in height and require moist, well-drained, peaty soil and partial shade. Another treasure requiring similar conditions is the

Japanese *Kirengeshoma palmata*, with interesting palm-like leaves covered with greyish hairs, borne on branching 3- to 4-foot stems. The terminal clusters of pendulous, bell-shaped, yellow flowers have a gleaming lustrous texture that always evokes comment. These last two plants extend the interest in the woodland into late summer and autumn long after the burst of spring and summer flowers.

Some of the paeony species are beautiful when grown in the wild garden in light shade. Pride of place should perhaps go to the bright butter yellow *Paeonia mlokosewitschii* or the rather similar *P. wittmanniana*. Both have bluish-green foliage, which is a delight after the flowers have faded.

Moisture-loving Plants

A stream, pool, or even a low-lying ditch provide an excellent opportunity to grow a wide range of plants of great beauty. Kingcups (*Caltha palustris*) are one of the miracles of spring, with their brilliant golden flowers when massed in damp places. Both the single and double forms are of easy cultivation. Lysichitums, or skunk cabbages as they are familiarly known, like similar conditions. The striking arum-like flowers which appear in early spring, yellow for *Lysichitum americanum* and white for the more difficult *L. camtschatcense*, are followed by huge cabbage-like leaves 1 to 2½ feet tall (Plate 11). Gunneras have probably the largest leaves of all moisture-loving plants and must be grown with their feet in water by the pond-side or in a bog.

Candelabra primulas like damp, leafy soil in sun or partial shade. They come in a wonderful array of colours – rose, crimson, orange, apricot, yellow, and white. They may be grown from seed sown when ripe in a pan or box of John Innes Seed Compost. They may be slow to germinate, but by late the following spring the seedlings will be large enough to prick out in frames or boxes and then planted out in their permanent homes in August or early September to flower the following spring. Best known is the purplish-red *Primula japonica*, with its whorls of flowers borne on scapes 1½ to 3 feet tall. There are named forms like 'Miller's Crimson' and 'Postford White'. *P. pulverulenta* is another fine easy primula for moist conditions. The deep-red flowers are borne

132. *Iris sibirica* used for waterside planting.

133. *Astilbe* 'Gladstone' in a moist position.

in whorls on 3-foot scapes which are covered with a silvery farinose bloom. There is the fine pink Bartley Strain and named cultivars like 'Red Hugh' and 'Lady Thursby'. In the orange range there are *P. bulleyana*, *chungensis*, and *cockburniana* and the glorious yellow *P. helodoxa*. All these require similar conditions and have a long flowering season. If various species are planted there can be a flowering period from mid-May, starting with *P. japonica* and extending through July as the whorls of flowers obligingly bloom several at a time.

Moisture-loving irises include the many forms of *Iris sibirica*, which send up flower stems among the long, grassy leaves to a height of 3 to 4 feet in June, with showy flowers in shades of violet, blue, purple and white, (Plate 132,) the rich violet-purple *I. delavayi*, and the superb Japanese irises (*I. kaempferi* and *I. laevigata*), which make a dazzling display in July with their wonderful blended colours and curious markings. The last two are both

134. The exotic flowers of the little used *Arisaema candidissimum*.

lime-haters and require a great deal of moisture in the growing season. *I. kaempferi* does not like to be too wet in winter, but *I. laevigata* grows with its feet in the water throughout the year.

Later in the summer there are the lovely monkey flowers or musks, the golden yellow *Mimulus luteus* being the best known. This plant requires plenty of moisture, but the many varieties of *M. cupreus*, including 'Whitecroft Scarlet', 'Red Emperor', 'Cerise Queen', and 'Bees' Dazzler', described as pillar-box red, require less-moist conditions. In their demands they resemble the showy astilbes, which are equally at home in a cool, rich border or by the side of a pond. Rich soil and partial shade are essential. Being relatively surface-rooting, astilbes do not like hot, dry positions. Propagate them by division in early autumn or spring, and as they are heavy feeders give them an annual mulch of rich compost or well-rotted manure. Colours, which range from white to pink, lilac, red, and crimson, may be selected from the many named clones described in plant catalogues. (Plate 133.)

135. *Iris* 'White City'.

12 · Essential Herbaceous Plants

Space does not permit a detailed discussion of a great number of the more familiar genera found in the herbaceous border, but details are necessary about a few of the more essential ones, common to most gardens. These include irises, delphiniums, paeonies, lupins, Michaelmas daisies, and phlox, and of course dahlias and chrysanthemums deserve a place. All these plants are suited to cutting beds and borders as well as to decorative borders, but the methods of cultivation are essentially the same wherever they are grown. Lists of recommended varieties will be found in the Appendices.

Irises

Among the most spectacular of all hardy herbaceous plants are the bearded irises (Plates 135, 136), which bring bold masses of colour to borders and shrubberies in May and June before most other border plants have flowered. The range of colours is wide, including clear self colours, subtle blends, and strongly contrasting ones where the standards and falls are different. Irises are easy to grow, being amenable to both town and country gardens. The two prerequisites are sun and perfect drainage. This does not mean that irises cannot be grown in half shade. They will thrive, but they will not flower as freely, and will lack much of the stamina of plants grown in full sun. Drainage must be good, or the fleshy rhizomes tend to rot.

Irises grow best in beds by themselves where other plants do not crowd them or shade their roots. However, they are very effective in clumps along the front of shrubberies (Plate 137) and herbaceous borders. Irises are relatively fragile flowers and need protection from strong winds, especially the new taller varieties.

Irises can be planted any time after they finish flowering in June or early July. But later July and early August is not a good time, as the rhizomes are making their major root growth. Late August and September are excellent, and obviously the sooner the plants settle down in their permanent home, the more quickly they make

136. The clear blue *Iris* 'Jane Phillips'.

root growth, and flowering the following year is assured. Spring planting is possible but not recommended, as irises seldom flower that year.

Dig the soil deeply well in advance of planting time so that it has time to consolidate. If the soil is heavy the bed should be raised several inches or more above the ground level. On the whole, avoid manure, save on very light, poor soils, as it tends to promote vigorous root and leaf growth rather than flower-heads. It also encourages both stem and rhizome rot. Humus, however, is essential. It can be supplied by generous amounts of well-rotted garden compost or leaf mould, and where these are not available

137. Irises and columbines bordering a paved path offer an interesting
contrast of foliage forms.

138. The rhizomes of irises in early August with one, two, and three fans, the last having borne a flower stem, now removed. Note dark old roots and lighter new ones.

granulated peat or hop manure is admirable. Irises like lime, and this is best provided in the form of old mortar rubble, especially on heavy soils, where ashes, coarse sand, limestone chippings, or gravel should also be used to promote good drainage. Work coarse bone meal and a sprinkling of sulphate of potash into the surface as food. The former is slow to break down, but it has a lasting effect.

Planting should be shallow, with the surface of the rhizome exposed to the sun. Cut off the foliage 6 inches from the base so that the rhizome will sit more firmly in the soil (Plate 138). Dip the cut edges in a weak solution of potassium permanganate (1 teaspoonful to a quart of water) to prevent the entry of fungus infection. Set the plants at least a foot apart, allowing 15 to 18 inches where plants with multiple fans are used. All fans should face the same way, preferably south. Place the rhizome on the surface of the soil and take out a small trench on either side to accommodate the roots. Cover them so that only the top of the rhizome is left above the ground. Firm the soil carefully and make sure that the fan is not subsequently dislodged. On heavy soils it is advisable to use a few inches of coarse sand to form the mound which supports the rhizome. With irises planted in late June or early July root action follows quickly. In August long roots will have already developed, and these complicate planting. They must on no account be shortened, or the vital hair roots are removed. After planting has been completed make sure the bed is level so that water does not collect in low areas.

Irises should be lifted and divided every third year, but much will depend on how closely the rhizomes were originally placed, the vigour of the variety, and the nature of the soil. Careful dividing and the re-making of the bed with the incorporation of new humus pays dividends in both the quality and quantity of the flowers. An annual feeding with bone meal after flowering is beneficial, and a handful of well-broken-down leaf mould tucked in around the growing end of each rhizome is recommended by a great iris authority.

Delphiniums

Delphiniums (Plates 139, 140) deserve a place in almost every hardy border, and they are lovely when grown in a bed on their own, with perhaps a border of nepeta or pinks. They are also superb for the cutting garden or the kitchen garden, where they can be grown in rows or blocks. Give delphiniums an airy, sunny position, protected if possible from prevailing winds. Rich soil is essential for good results, and there must be adequate moisture, especially in July and August. These two requirements necessitate a large quantity of humus in the soil to ensure food for hungry roots and water retention. Very acid soil is not suitable, nor is heavy, wet clay, which encourages black rot.

Deep cultivation is essential. Double dig and if possible work a liberal quantity of well-decomposed manure into the lower spit and incorporate some in the upper one as well. Specialists often remove the soil and mix it with manure and leaf mould before replacing it. A balanced fertilizer containing nitrates, potash, and phosphates mixed with leaf compost or hops can be used where

139. *Delphinium* 'Dame Myra Curtis'.

140. *Delphinium* 'Sutton's White'.

organic fertilizer is not available. Allow the soil to settle before planting, or consolidate it by treading and then lightly re-working the surface. As delphiniums are heavy feeders, clumps should be lifted every three or four years, the soil re-made, and new stock planted. Mulching in late April or early May is beneficial, as it both feeds and helps to retain the moisture in the border in the dry summer months. A bi-weekly dose of manure water from early May through the flowering season works wonders. ·

Propagation is by the three usual methods – seed sowing, cuttings, and division. Seeds should be sown from January to early March in a greenhouse, or July in seed boxes in a frame or shed where they are shielded from the sun until after germination. Sowing in the open ground or an open frame in July or August is also recommended. Prick out the young seedlings when large enough to handle into boxes of loose compost about 2 inches apart and harden them off. When large enough move them into beds in the open ground, placing them about 9 inches or a foot apart unless they are to remain there permanently. Although the earlier planted seeds will flower in August or September, strengthen the plants and encourage side growths by removal of the flower growths. The following spring move the plants to their final position. Cuttings (Plates 141–3) should be taken from February to early April. Leave the strongest shoots to flower, but remove the next best shoots when 3 to 4 inches long, scraping away earth from the root so that if possible a bit of the hard wood may be taken as a heel (see p. 102). Plants produced from cuttings will usually flower in August. For propagation by division see p. 100.

The new Giant Pacific Strain of delphiniums which are becoming so popular are best treated as biennials, and seeds should be sown every year or two. There are no named cultivars as with British delphiniums, but instead colour groups or series. These include Galahad (whites with white eyes), Astolat (very pale pinks), Black Knight (dark violet and purple), and blues, which include Summer Skies and Blue Jay. British delphiniums generally (Plate 139) have the asset of greater hardiness and, of course, are obtainable as named cultivars. Care should be taken in selection to ensure that varieties fulfil the requirements of your site as to size and habit, some being too tall for smaller gardens. The Bella-

141. Removing cuttings from parent plant.

142. Prepared cuttings taken with a heel being inserted around edge of a pot of compost.

143. Cuttings with a layer of sand to prevent rotting ready to be placed in a covered frame or box after watering.

144. A delphinium showing the effects of spring frosts and winds rather than of disease as one might suspect. This condition will right itself.

donna hybrids are beautiful smaller plants producing multiple flower stems 2½ to 3 feet tall. Cultivars include 'Capri', 'Isis', 'Wendy', 'Blue Bees', 'Lamartine', and 'Naples'. (See Appendix B for general list of good garden varieties of delphiniums.)

Delphiniums need careful thinning, as old-established clumps will send up too many spikes. Of course, the more rigorous the thinning, the larger the remaining ones. Staking is essential (see p. 88 and Plates 54, 55). The great enemy of delphiniums is the slug. On many soils this menace is so real that spring planting is advised. For control see p.135. Collars may also be used to advantage. Delphiniums are sometimes subject to black rot and black spot, especially on cold, wet soil. For these no satisfactory control has been found. In wet seasons mildew may be bothersome, but it can be controlled by a lime sulphur spray (see p. 138).

After flowering cut off the flower-head, leaving the lower stalk and leaves. In herbaceous borders other plants may be trained through them. New growths will be produced in most localities. A third flowering should be discouraged in areas where this is possible, as it weakens the plants.

145. *Paeonia* 'Globe of Light' with pink petals and golden staminodes.

Paeonies

Paeonies are most useful, as they are equally suited to the herbaceous border, shrubberies, the cutting garden, or to beds on their own. They are hardy, attractive throughout the growing season, and ideal for cutting. Their foliage is lovely in early spring, when the bronze or brilliant red curled leaves break the surface of the brown earth, and in autumn, when the foliage turns rich hues of purple and scarlet. The season lasts through May and June and sometimes into early July, later of course in cool districts. They are easy of cultivation if certain basic principles are followed, and they are relatively free from disease.

The earliest paeonies are the species and their varieties, excluding the *albiflora* or *lactiflora* group, in which most of the large June-flowered hybrids (Plates 145, 146) are classed. These hybrids are also known as Chinese paeonies (consult Appendix C for best varieties). The so-called tree paeonies though not herbaceous are among the finest plants for the mixed shrub border. Of the early May-flowering paeonies the best known are *Paeonia officinalis* and its varieties, including the double rose and the old double red

146. The very dark crimson *Paeonia* 'Defender'.

known as *rosea plena* and *rubra plena* respectively, the clear butter-yellow bowl-shaped *P. mlokosewitschii* (cover illustration), the paler yellow *P. wittmanniana*, and the brilliant single *P. peregrina*, usually listed in catalogues as 'Fire King' and 'Sunbeam'.

Paeonies like a good position in sun or light shade where the soil is deep and drainage good. They will grow in the shade of cherries, crabs, and plums, but the dense shade of forest trees like oaks, beeches, and sycamores is unfavourable. They are happy on either acid or alkaline soil as long as it is not too extreme. The soil should be deeply dug and copiously manured or treated with compost or leaf mould. Borders and beds should be prepared well in advance and allowed to settle. For individual clumps a hole 2 feet deep and as much across is none too big to prepare, and it will pay dividends in future. In borders allow 2 to 4 feet between plants, depending on the vigour of the variety. For the large June-flowering ones 3 or 4 feet is not too much, as they resent distur-bance and should not be moved. The best planting season is September or the first half of October, but on light, warm soils later planting is possible.

Plant firmly, making sure that the crown is not more than 2 inches at most below the surface. This is important. New plants should be well watered in. Keep them well watered the first season, as failure is often caused by drought before they have established. On light soils a winter mulch is beneficial. The dead leaves can afford a useful protection. The first year it is better not to let the plants flower, great as the temptation may be to see them. Subse-quently disbud if giant blooms are required. If side buds are left the season is prolonged and the show of bloom is more spectacu-lar. Paeonies are best staked either with brush or metal guard rings (see p. 88 and Plate 48).

Diseases of paeonies are not prevalent. They are occasionally subject to botrytis in wet seasons. This is detected by a purple coloration of the stems and a withering of leaves. It can be con-trolled by spraying when first detected with a solution of Bor-deaux Mixture, but seriously infected foliage should be burnt. Copper lime dust is also effective. Ants are often seen on the stems and buds of paeonies, but they do no harm.

147. Russell lupins growing in a bed bordered with nepeta.

Lupins

Few perennials offer such a dazzling range of colours as the modern hybrids known collectively as Russell lupins (Plate 147). They are easy to grow, thriving in full sun or semi-shade on light, loamy soils. They are particularly suited to town gardens where space permits. They flower in June and early July with such profusion that borders devoted to them become rivers of colour, and in mixed herbaceous borders they provide the first major display along with the oriental poppies, anchusas, and paeonies. Russell lupins are of two types – self-coloured and bi-colours with the keel (bell) and wings contrasting (Plate 148). To the former group belong the creamy white 'Alicia Parrett', 'Apple Blossom', 'Canary Bird', and the violet-blue 'Thundercloud'; to the latter, the mauve and white 'Lilac Time', the terra-cotta and yellow 'Fred Yule', and the coral and creamy yellow 'George Russell' (consult Appendix D for good garden varieties). Tree lupins are excellent for the mixed border and flower in their second year. The colour range is restricted to yellow, white, and mauve.

194

148. Two spikes of self-coloured lupins with a bicolour on the right.

Lupins are easy of cultivation and comparatively disease-free as long as plants are healthy. Old plants deteriorate rapidly. Lupins dislike lime. On chalky soils special beds of neutral or slightly acid soil should be prepared. Do not overfeed, as lupins, unlike delphiniums, do not react well to a rich diet. Save on poor soils, the use of extra manure should be avoided. Heavy soils are not satisfactory unless the drainage is improved, as the plants grow less vigorously and deteriorate rapidly.

As lupins are short lived, renew them at intervals of three or four years. Lupins will flower from seed in twelve months, but seeds will not come true, and for named clones, vegetative propagation is essential. However, very attractive ones of a given colour such as rose or yellow can be grown from seed. Take 3- to 4-inch cuttings with a bit of the woody root-stock as a heel in March or April and root them in a closed frame. Division of lupins is possible, but it must be carefully done, preferably in spring. All woody spent growth should be carefully cut out and the growths with young fibrous roots planted with the crown well below the surface. Firm planting is essential. New stock from nurseries should preferably be planted in spring. Allow 2 to 2½ feet between plants and make bold clumps of a single variety.

Lupins should be staked if planted in exposed conditions, but well-grown plants in a border are usually sturdy enough to support themselves. After flowering the seed pods should be removed at the foot of the flower-head. If seeds are to be gathered save a single stalk or two, remembering, of course, that the seeds will not necessarily come true.

Michaelmas Daisies

This term is applied to a wide number of members of the genus *Aster*. The largest group are hybrids of *Aster novi-belgi*, but others, such as 'Harrington's Pink' and 'Barr's Pink', derive from *A. novae-angliae*, and there is the striking *A. amellus* group, best known of which are 'King George', 'Sonia', 'Ultramarine', and 'Moorheim Gem'. There are other types, but space does not permit an account here. Of the *novi-belgii* group there are plants of varying colours, heights, and habits for many positions, from mounded dwarfs like 'Audrey', 'Margaret Rose' (Plate 149),

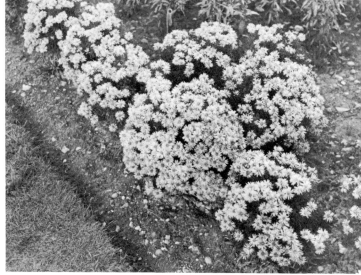

149. The dwarf pink *Aster* 'Margaret Rose' needs no support.

and 'Snow Sprite', little more than 10 to 18 inches high, to the taller 'Peace' (Plate 150) 'Ada Ballard', 'Gayborder Royal', 'Cardinal', and 'Mount Everest', ranging in height from 3 to 4 feet. The colours are superb, with enormous variation in the white, pink, blue, mauve, purple, and red range. Recently there have been glowing ruby reds like 'Winston S. Churchill' and the rosy crimson of 'Beechwood Beacon'. (For good varieties consult Appendix E.)

The flower season is a fairly long one, the *amellus* group starting in July, and the bulk of the others starting spasmodically in early August, working up to a crescendo in late August and mid-September, and trailing off into October. They are definitely late summer and autumn flowers.

All types like sun and air. They are not particular as to soil, but require feeding and moderate moisture for best results. Michaelmas daisies are a little like phloxes as far as their root systems are concerned, as both are fibrous and spreading, but so vigorous are most varieties that they quickly form densely matted clumps and deteriorate in quality unless divided every third year. All varieties can be divided in autumn or spring save the *A. amellus* group,

150. *Aster* 'Peace', one of the best known of all Michaelmas daisies.

which can be lifted only in spring. Propagation is very simple, as most of them spread freely by underground fibrous root-stocks. The best of these should be used and the tired centres of old plants discarded. Excellent plants can be grown from cuttings taken in spring and rooted in a closed frame. These should be used for specimen plants or widely spaced groups where the form of individual plants are the objective rather than a solid mass of colour.

Taller varieties and those with large individual flowers will require staking. Pea sticks are excellent or patented supports (see p. 88 and Plate 95). The dwarf varieties are solid, of good habit and need no staking (Plate 149).

151. A truss of the lilac-mauve *Phlox* 'Undine'.

Phloxes

These are the glory of the summer border from early July until late September, although they reach their peak in August. Border phloxes (Plate 151, 152) are generally forms of *Phlox decussata* (*paniculata*), ranging in height from 1½ to 4 feet. Colours are unbelievably rich, particularly in the case of recent introductions. White phlox is attractive in the summer border, but there are varying shades of pink, red, scarlet, mauve, and purple. As yet there is no true blue phlox, but there are several lavenders that approach it. Many phloxes have pips (the individual flowers) with an eye of a different colour. Phloxes are treasured almost as much for their scent as for their colours. Well-grown plants are sufficiently sturdy so that no staking is required.

For success with phlox certain conditions are essential. First and foremost they must be grown in rich, well-drained soil with plenty of moisture in the growing season. They thrive either in full sun or light shade. A rich, sandy soil into which plenty of humus in the form of well-rotted manure, leaf mould, spent hops, or garden compost has been incorporated is ideal. Humus must be present not only as food but also to hold the moisture. In dry weather phlox must be given a thorough soaking every few days, or it will be of poor quality, with yellow foliage and small, sparsely flowered trusses.

The dreaded enemy of phlox is eelworm. Its presence may be detected by the yellowing of the leaves coupled with twisting and by the shrunken, contorted stems, which in time rot. Infected plants must be burnt, as there is no safe remedy. However, it is possible to propagate from the roots of infected plants, as the eelworms are only present in the stems and woody crowns. Cuttings from clean, fibrous roots several inches in length may be inserted obliquely in drills in a sandy compost in a covered pot, box, or frame. These should be covered to a depth of an inch or more and kept well watered until surface growth appears (see p. 106). At this point they should be planted out in good compost. Phloxes are easily propagated by division, but all old woody spent growths from the centre of established clumps should be discarded in favour of the outer bits with good, fleshy, fibrous roots.

Phlox should be planted in bold clumps. Personally I do not like mixing several colours in a group, but it is often done. An occasional feeding with liquid manure when the plants are making flower-buds works wonders. In old clumps the shoots may be thinned in spring, healthy ones being used for cuttings and the best ones left to develop. This will ensure larger, stronger trusses rather than a great number of smaller ones. Phloxes should be lifted every three or four years so that the soil can be properly enriched. It then is wise to plant new stock. When plants are purchased make sure that only good clean stocks are provided. Phlox should be planted 12 to 18 inches apart.

152. Phloxes in a summer border.

Appendices

APPENDIX A · Tall Bearded Iris (*Iris germanica*)
Abbreviations: ST, *standard;* F, *fall*

Amoenas (ST white or near
   white, F coloured)
Braithwaite
Pinnacle
Wabash

Black
Black Forest
Black Hills
Sable

Blends (Blended colours,
   including yellow)
Benton Cordelia
Lady Mohr
Mary Randall
Starshine
Melbreak

Blue
Arabi Pasha
Blue Ensign
Blue Shimmer
Blue Valley
Chivalry
Derwentwater
Great Lakes
Harbour Blue
Helen McGregor
Jane Phillips
Sierra Skies
South Pacific

Brown
Argus Pheasant

Inca Chief
Tarn Hows
Troutbeck

Lavender
Blumohr
Frances Craig

Pink
Chérie
Dreamcastle
Happy Birthday
Pink Formal
Rose Splendour
Strathmore

Plicatas (White or yellow ground
   with stippling or feathering of
   blue, pink, red, or brown)
Belle Meade
Benton Daphne
Blue Shimmer
Firecracker

Variegatas (ST yellow or
   orange, F contrasting)
Gay Head
Staten Island

Red
Carnton
Quebec
Technicolor

White
Arctic Snow

Cliffs of Dover
Kanchenjunga
New Snow
Snow Flurry
White City

Yellow
Buttermere

Cloth of Gold
Desert Song
Golden Alps
Mattie Gates
Moonlight Sonata
Ola Kala
Spell Binder
Truly Yours
Zantha

APPENDIX B · Delphiniums – Elatum Type and Belladonna

All varieties are 5 to 6 feet unless noted

Agnes Brooks – gentian blue, with white eye

Alice Artindale – double, lilac blue

Anona – pale blue, tinged mauve, white eye

Beau Nash – semi-double, deep purple, black and gold eye

Blackmore's Blue – semi-double, sky-blue with white eye

Blackmore's Glorious – semi-double, sky-blue and mauve, white eye

Blue Bees (Belladonna) – single, pale blue, white eye, 3 to 4 ft

Blue Lagoon – good blue, semi-double

C. F. Langdon – semi-double, pure blue, black eye

C. H. Middleton – semi-double, medium blue, sulphur eye

Capri (Belladonna) – sky blue, 3 ft

Crystal – semi-double, sky-blue, white eye

Dame Myra Curtis – sky-blue, semi-double, blue and black eye

Duchess of Portland – semi-double, ultramarine blue, white eye

Edward Bromet – deep violet-blue, white eye

Isis (Belladonna) – semi-double, purplish blue, 3 ft

Jennifer Langdon – semi-double, pale blue and mauve, black eye

Lady Eleanor – double, sky-blue

Lamartine (Belladonna) – single, dark violet-blue, 3 ft

Lorna – semi-double, rich blue, brown eye

Moerheimi (Belladonna) – white, 3 to 4 ft

Mrs Frank Bishop – gentian-blue

Naples (Belladonna) – brilliant blue, semi-double, 3 to 4 ft

Orion (Belladonna) – cornflower-blue, 3 ft

Pink Sensation (Belladonna) – single, light pink, 3 ft

Purple Prince – semi-double, rich purple, white eye

Pyramus – semi-double, rich blue, shaded mauve, white eye

Sir Neville Pearson – semi-double, deep purple-blue, black eye
W. B. Cranfield – semi-double, deep mauve and blue

Wendy (Belladonna) – gentian-blue, $3\frac{1}{2}$ ft
W. R. Chaplain – semi-double, deep mauve

APPENDIX C · Paeonies (*Paeonia lactiflora*)

Doubles

Adolphe Rousseau – maroon-red
Alice Harding – pale amber on white ground
Baroness Schroeder – pale flesh-white to snow-white
Claire Dubois – light satiny pink
Duchesse de Nemours – sulphur white to pure white
James Kelway – blush white to milk white
Joy of Life – semi-double, pink and white
Kelway's Glorious – pure white
Kelway's Lovely – bright rose
Lady Alexandra Duff – delicate blush-pink
Laura Dessert – creamy white, canary-yellow centre
Marie Crousse – soft coral pink, turning white
Mons. Charles Leveque – silvery blush-pink to white
Mons. Jules Elie – silver lavender to white
Phyllis Kelway – rose-pink, paling to white in centre
Primavera – blush-white, pale yellow petaloids

Sarah Bernhardt – apple-blossom pink
Thérèse – white, flushed blush-pink
Walter Favon – bright rose-pink

Singles

Bowl of Beauty – rose with yellow staminodes
Defender – deep crimson, very large
Duchess of Sutherland – flesh-pink to white
E. St Hill – pale pink
English Elegance – faint blush-pink
Globe of Light – pure rose, gold centre
Lord Kitchener – dazzling maroon-red
Mikado – deep carmine, old gold and maroon petaloid centre
Nymph – pale pink
Orion – deep crimson, tall
Pride of Langport – brilliant rosy pink
Whitleyi – blush turning pure white
Wilbur Wright – black-red or chocolate

204

APPENDIX D · Russell Lupins

All heights 3 to 4 feet save where noted.
Abbreviations: κ, *keel;* w, *wings*

Apple Blossom – pink self

Beryl Viscountess Cowdray – κ cerise-red, w crimson

Betty Astell – Bright pink

Blue Jacket – κ deep blue, w white

Canary Bird – canary-yellow self

Cherry Pie – κ cherry-red, w carmine with yellow, fading ivory

City of York – κ bright red, w deep red, flushed orange

Daydream – κ peach pink, w golden yellow

Elsie Waters – κ bright pink, w cream, edged pink

Fantasy – κ creamy yellow, w rose-pink

Fireglow – κ bright orange, w orange flushed gold

George Russell – κ coral pink, w creamy yellow, edged pink

Gladys Cooper – κ slate-blue, w pinkish mauve

Heather Glow – κ wine-red, w bronze

Joan of York – κ cerise, w white

Lady Diana Abdy – κ sky-blue, w white, flushed blue

Lilac Time – κ rosy lilac, w cream, flushed mauve

Mrs Garnet Botfield – pure deep yellow

Mrs Micklethwaite – κ salmon-pink, w pale gold, shaded red

My Love – rich cream

Rita – κ deep carmine, w rosy carmine

Thundercloud – κ violet-purple, w violet, flushed mauve

Tom Reeves – pure deep yellow

Wheatsheaf – deep golden yellow

APPENDIX E · Perennial Asters

Aster amellus (Spring planting only)

Advance – violet-blue, 2 ft, Sept.–Oct.

Bessie Chapman – violet-blue, 2½ ft, Aug.–Oct.

Blue King – violet-blue, 2½ ft, Sept.

Blue Star – deep blue, 2 ft, Aug.–Sept.

Jaqueline Genebrier – bright pink, 2½ ft, Aug.–Sept.

Frikartii – lavender-blue, 3 ft, Aug.–Oct.

King George – violet-blue, 2 ft, July–Sept.

Lady Hindlip – deep pink, 2½ ft, Aug.–Oct.

Mauve Beauty – 2–3 ft, Sept.–Oct.

Moerheim Gem – deep blue, 2 ft, Aug.–Oct.

Mrs Ralph Woods – rose-pink, 2½ ft, Aug.–Oct.

Nocturne – rosy-lavender, 2½ ft, Aug.–Oct.

Red Fire – deep red, 2 ft, Aug.–Oct.

Sonia – bright pink, 2 ft, Aug.–Oct.

Ultramarine – violet-blue, $2\frac{1}{2}$ ft, Aug.– Oct.

Vanity – violet-blue, $2\frac{1}{2}$ ft, Aug.– Oct.

Aster novae-angliae (Late August to September unless noted)

Barr's Blue – purplish blue, 4 ft

Barr's Pink – bright pink, 4 ft

Crimson Beauty – rosy crimson, October, 4 ft

Harrington's Pink – clear pink, $4\frac{1}{2}$ ft

Incomparabilis – fuchsia-purple, $2\frac{1}{2}$ ft

Red Cloud – rosy red, $3\frac{1}{2}$ ft

William Bowman – rosy purple, 5 ft

Aster novi-belgii (Taller varieties, flowering September to October)

Ada Ballard – mauvy blue, 3 ft

Alaska – white, $2\frac{1}{2}$ ft

Apple Blossom – delicate pink, 3 to 4 ft

Archbishop – very large, semi-double, purple-blue, $3\frac{1}{2}$ ft

Beachwood Beacon – Rosy crimson, 3 ft

Beechwood Rival – ruby-red, 3 to 4 ft

Bishop – plum-purple, very large, $3\frac{1}{2}$ ft

Blandie – white, semi-double, 4 to 5 ft

Blue Eyes – lavender-blue, 4 ft

Blue Gown – clear blue, very late, 5 ft, Oct.

Chequers – rich violet-purple, 2 ft

Crimson Brocade – double, rich red, 3 ft

Dawn – semi-double, light pink, 3 ft

Dean – pink, $3\frac{1}{2}$ ft

Ernest Ballard – semi-double, rich crimson-pink, 3 ft

Eventide – large, semi-double, violet-blue, 3 ft

Fellowship – pink, 3 ft

F. M. Simpson – large purple-blue, $2\frac{1}{2}$ ft

Gayborder Blue – bright blue, 4 ft

Gayborder Royal – bright purplish-crimson, 3 ft

Harrison's Blue – amethyst-blue, $3\frac{1}{2}$ ft

Hilda Ballard – rosy lilac, semi-double, 4 ft

Janet McMullen – Semi-double, rosy pink, 4 ft

Lassie – pale rosy-pink, 4 ft

Little Boy Blue – bright blue, double, $2\frac{1}{2}$ ft

Little Pink Lady – double, pink, $2\frac{1}{2}$ ft

Marie Ballard – powder blue, double, 3 to 4 ft

Melbourne Belle – deep rose, compact, 2 ft

Melbourne Magnet – soft blue, semi-double, $3\frac{1}{2}$ ft

Moderator – dark, violet-purple, $3\frac{1}{2}$ ft

Peace – rosy mauve, large, $3\frac{1}{2}$ ft

Peerless – heliotrope, semi-double, 4 ft

Picture – pale crimson, 4 ft

Plenty – semi-double, light mauve, 4 ft

Rector – claret-red, $3\frac{1}{2}$ ft
Red Sunset – rosy crimson, $3\frac{1}{2}$ ft
Royal Velvet – violet, full, $3\frac{1}{2}$ ft
White Wings – single white, 4 ft
Winston Churchill – ruby crimson, 2 to $2\frac{1}{2}$ ft

Aster novi-belgii (Dwarf varieties, flowering September to October)
Audrey – lilac-mauve, 15 in.
Autumn Princess – semi-double, lavender-blue, 15 in.
Blue Bouquet – violet-blue, 12 in.

Countess of Dudley – shell-pink, 18 in.
Jean – rich violet-mauve, $1\frac{1}{2}$ to 2 ft
Lilac Time – clear lilac, 12 in.
Little Pink Pyramid – rose pink, 18 in.
Little Red Boy – rosy-red, 12 in.
Margaret Rose – pink, 12 in.
Pink Lace – double, pink, 15 in.
Queen of Sheba – soft pink on lilac, 10 in.
Rosebud – semi-double, deep rose, 15 in.
Snowsprite – dwarf white, 12 in.
Victor – light blue, 9 in.

APPENDIX F · Border Phloxes (*Phlox paniculata* or *P. decussata*)

Heights $2\frac{1}{2}$ to 3 feet unless noted

Admiral – deep red
A. E. Amos – bright scarlet
Amethyst – deep lavender-blue
Annie Laurie – salmon pink
Border Gem – petunia-purple
Brigadier – vivid orange-red
B. Symons-Jeune – rosy pink, carmine eye, $3\frac{1}{2}$ ft
Caroline van den Berg – lavender-blue
Cecil Hanbury – orange-salmon, carmine eye
Charles H. Curtis – brilliant red
Daily Sketch – salmon-pink, carmine eye
Dresden China – soft shell pink
Everest – fine pure white
Fanal – deep purplish red
Frau Ant. Buchner – pure white

Glamis – bright pink, purple eye
Graf Zeppelin – large white, carmine eye
Iceberg – white, shaded violet
Jules Sandeau – pure pink
Lord Lambourne – carmine-pink, white eye
Mia Ruys – white, dwarf, 2 ft
Mother of Pearl – white, suffused pink, 2 ft
Pink Gown – pure pink
Rembrandt – pure white
Salmon Glow – strong pink, shaded salmon
Sandringham – rosy purple, bright eye
Sir John Falstaff – salmon-pink, purple eye

207

Spitfire – Salmon shaded orange
Toits de Paris – soft lavender-blue, 2 ft

Undine – lilac-mauve
Windsor – light cerise, carmine eye

APPENDIX G · Plants for Cutting

This list does not attempt to enumerate all the possible species and varieties but to point out the most important genera

Acanthus
Achillea filipendulina 'Gold Plate'
Achillea millefolium
Achillea ptarmica
Aconitum
Alstroemeria
Anthemis
Artemisia lactiflora
Aster amellus
Aster cordifolius
Aster ericoides
Aster novi-belgii
Aster yunnanensis 'Napsbury'
Astrantia
Campanula glomerata dahurica
Campanula latifolia
Campanula persicifolia
Chrysanthemum maximum
Chrysanthemum rubellum
Convallaria majalis
Coreopsis
Delphinium
Dianthus
Doronicum
Echinops
Eremurus
Erigeron
Eryngium
Gaillardia
Gypsophila paniculata
Helenium
Helianthus
Heliopsis
Helleborus niger
Hemerocallis
Heuchera
Kniphofia
Liatris
Limonium
Lychnis chalcedonica
Paeonia
Papaver
Penstemons
Phlox paniculata
Physalis
Polyanthus
Pyrethrum
Ranunculus
Rudbeckia
Scabiosa caucasica
Sedum spectabile
Solidago
Trollius
Viola

APPENDIX H · Flowers and Seed Heads for Drying for Winter

Acanthus mollis
Acanthus spinosus
Achillea filipendulina 'Gold Plate'
Anaphalis triplinervis
Cynara cardunculus (Cardoon)
Delphinium

208

Dictamnus albus (seed pods)
Echinops
Eryngium
Gypsophila paniculata
Iris foetidissima (seed heads), *ochroleuca* (seed pods)
Lilium giganteum (seed pods)

Limonium
Onoopordon
Paeonia mlokosewitschii (seed heads)
Papaver orientale (seed pods)
Physalis
Stachys lanata

APPENDIX I · Plants for Ground Cover

A few of shrubby habit have been included though not strictly herbaceous

Ajuga reptans atropurpurea – semi-shade, 6 to 12 inches

Alchemilla alpina – sun, half-shade, 5 in.

Alchemilla mollis – sun, half-shade, 18 in.

Asarum europaeum – creeping evergreen, shade, 3 in.

Asperula odorata (Woodruff) – delicate cover, shade, 6 in.

Bergenia – all species and hybrids, sun or shade, 9 to 18 in.

Brunnera macrophylla – half to full shade, 18 in.

Convallaria majalis – (Lily of the valley), 9 in.

Cornus canadensis – sandy peaty soil, moist shady position, 6 in.

Epimedium – all species and hybrids, sun or shade, 9 to 12 in.

Geranium endressii – sun or semi-shade, 18 in.

Geranium grandiflorum alpinum – sun or semi-shade, 12 in.

Geranium macrorrhizum – sun or shade, 12 in.

Geranium nodosum – shade if not too dry, 12 in.

Hemerocallis – sun or semi-shade, 2 to 3 ft

Heucherella tiarelloides – sun or partial shade, 18 in.

Hostas – in variety, weed-proof covers, semi-shade, 1 to 2 ft

Hypericum calycinum – evergreen, sun or shade, 12 in.

Iris foetidissima – sun or shade, 2 ft

Lamium galeobdolon variegatum – excellent rapid ground cover, sun or shade, 12 in.

Lysimachia nummularia (Creeping Jenny) – sun or shade, 6 in.

Mentha rotundifolia variegata – sun or half shade, moist, 2 ft

Nepeta faassenii (*mussinii*) – sun, 12 in.

Origanum vulgare aureum – sun, 9 in.

Polygonum affine – dense, sun or shade, 12 in.

Pulmonaria angustifolia – semi-shade, 9 in.

Pulmonaria saccharata – semi-shade, 9 in.

Saxifraga umbrosa (London Pride) – sun or shade, 9 in.

Stachys lanata – sun, evergreen grey carpeter, 6 in.

Symphytum grandiflorum – useful ground cover, semi-shade, 9 in.

Symphytum peregrinum – coarse ground cover, sun or partial shade, 3 ft

Tiarella cordifolia (Foam Flower) – semi-shade, 9 in.

Vinca major – evergreen, sun or shade, 18 in.

Vinca minor – evergreen, shade or semi-shade, 9 in.

APPENDIX J · Perennials for Chalky Soils

Acanthus mollis
Achillea ptarmica
Adenophora
Anchusa
Anemone hupehensis
Aquilegia vulgaris
Armeria
Asphodeline lutea
Campanula
Cheiranthus
Corydalis lutea
Crambe cordifolia
Dianthus
Doronicum
Echinops
Eremurus
Erigeron
Eryngium
Gaillardia
Geum
Gypsophila
Helenium

Helleborus orientalis
Hemerocallis
Iris germanica
Kentranthus
Kniphofia
Limonium
Linum perenne, narbonense
Lychnis chalcedonica
Malva
Oenothera
Ostrowskia
Papaver orientale
Pulsatilla
Romneya
Rudbeckia
Salvia
Scabiosa
Tradescantia
Verbascum
Veronica
Zauschneria

APPENDIX K · Plants for Dry, Sunny Positions

Achillea
Agastache (Brittonastrum)
Alstroemeria
Alyssum saxatile
Anaphalis
Anthemis
Antirrhinum asarina

Artemisia
Asphodeline
Baptisia
Buphthalmum salicifolium
Catananche caerulea
Centaurea
Cerastium tomentosum

Cichorium intybus
Echinops
Eryngium
Filipendula hexapetala
Gaillardia
Gaura
Gypsophila paniculata
Helichrysum angustifolium, trili-
neatum
Heliopsis
Hieracium
Hyssopus aristatus
Iris germanica, chamaeiris, pumila
Isatis glauca
Kentranthus (Valerian)
Lavatera olbia (Tree Mallow)
Limonium (Sea Lavender)

Linaria (Toadflax)
Lirum (Flax)
Lupins
Macleaya cordata (Bocconia)
Nepeta
Oenothera
Romneya coulteri, trichocalyx
Ruta graveolens
Saponaria officinalis flore pleno
Sedum
Solidago (Golden Rod)
Stachys lanata
Tanacetum (Tansy)
Thermopsis
Thymus
Verbascum (Mullein)
Zauschneria

APPENDIX L · Plants for Shady Positions

Many plants which will thrive in either sun or light shade are not
included. Plants marked * will tolerate heavy shade

Acanthus
Aconitum
*Actaea
Ajuga
Anemone hupehensis
Aquilegia
*Aruncus
*Asperula
*Astilbe
Astrantia
Bergenia
Campanula lactiflora, latifolia,
latiloba
*Cimicifuga
*Convallaria
Cynoglossum
*Dentaria
Dicentra
Digitalis

*Dodecatheon
Doronicum
*Epimedium
Euphorbia
*Galax
Gentiana asclepiadea
Geranium endressii, ibericum,
macrorrhizum
*Helleborus
Hemerocallis
*Hosta
Iris foetidissima
Kirengeshoma
Lamium galeobdolon variegatum,
maculatum aureum
Lobelia
Lysichitum
Lythrum
*Meconopsis

211

*Mertensia
Omphalodes
Peltiphyllum
Phlox
Physostegia
Polyanthus
*Polygonatum
Primula species
Pulmonaria
Rodgersia

Saxifraga umbrosa
*Smilacina
Symphytum
Thalictrum
*Tiarella
*Trillium
Tricyrtis
*Uvularia
Veratrum

APPENDIX M · Herbaceous Plants for Moist Positions

Aruncus sylvester
Astilbe
Caltha palustris
Cornus canadensis
Gunnera manicata
Hemerocallis
Hosta
Iris kaempferi
Iris laevigata
Iris ochroleuca
Iris pseudacorus
Iris sibirica
Kirengeshoma palmata
Lilium canadense
Lilium giganteum (*Cardiocrinum*)
Lilium pardalinum

Ligularia clivorum
Lobelia cardinalis
Lobelia syphilitica
Lysichitum americanum
Lysichitum camtschatense
Lysimachia
Mimulus
Peltiphyllum peltatum (*Saxifraga*)
Primula alpicola, beesiana, bulle-
   yana, cockburniana, denticulata,
   florindae, helodoxa, japonica,
   pulverulenta, rosea, sikkimensis
Rodgersia
Trollius
Veratrum

APPENDIX N · Plants for the Front of a Border or Small, Low Beds

Ajuga
Alchemilla mollis
Alyssum saxatile
Anthemis cupaniana
Armeria
Artemisia stelleriana
Asperula odorata

Aster novi-belgii dwarf forms
   (see p. 207)
Bergenia
Betonica grandiflora rosea
Brunnera macrophylla
Campanula carpatica
Campanula garganica

Campanula poscharskyana
Cheiranthus 'Harpur Crewe'
Cheiranthus 'Moonlight'
Corydalis lutea
Cynoglossum nervosum
Dianthus
Dicentra eximia
Dicentra formosa
Epimedium
Erigeron
Euphorbia epithymoides
Geranium endressii
Geranium grandiflorum alpinum
Geranium macrorrhizum
Geranium sanguineum
Geum
Gypsophila 'Rosy Veil'
Helianthemum (Rock Rose)
Heuchera brizoides hybrids
Heuchera sanguinea hybrids
Heucherella tiarelloides
Hosta
Iberis sempervirens
Incarvillea
Iris dwarf bearded and species
Libertia formosa
Limonium
Linum arboreum
Linum narbonense

Linum perenne
Lychnis viscaria flore pleno
Mentha rotundifolia variegata
Nepeta faassenii (mussinii)
Oenothera fruticosa 'Yellow River'
Oenothera missouriensis
Oenothera speciosa
Origanum vulgare aureum
Penstemon
Phlox stolonifera 'Blue Ridge'
Pinks
Polemonium
Polygonum affine
Polygonum bistorta superbum
Potentilla hybrids
Prunella grandiflora
Pulmonaria saccharata (shade)
Roscoea
Ruta 'Jackman's Blue'
Saxifraga umbrosa (London Pride)
Sedum spectabile
Stachys lanata
Veronica gentianoides
Veronica incana
Veronica spicata
Viola

APPENDIX O · Tall Plants for Large-scale Borders

Acanthus
Achillea filipendulina
Aconitum napellus, volubile, wilsonii
Artemisia lactiflora
Aruncus sylvester
Aster novae-angliae, novi-belgii
Campanula lactiflora
Cephalaria tartarica

Clematis heracleaefolia, davidiana, recta
Crambe cordifolia
Cynara scolymus glauca
Delphinium
Echinacea 'The King'
Eremurus
Eupatorium purpureum
Galega officinalis
Helenium

213

Helianthus
Heliopsis
Hollyhocks
Iris 'Monspur', *ochroleuca*
Lactuca plumieri
Lavatera olbia rosea
Ligularia
Macleaya cordata (Boconia)
Onoopordon acanthium
Rheum

Rodgersia
Romneya
Rudbeckia
Salvia ambigens, haematodes, uliginosa
Senecio macrophyllus, tanguticus
Thalictrum aquilegiifolium, dipterocarpum, glaucum
Verbascum
Verbena bonariensis

APPENDIX P · Plants for Foliage Effect

Flowers may also be a consideration

Acanthus mollis – sun

Achillea clypeolata – silvery, sun

Achillea taygetea – feathery grey, sun

Actaea spicata – green fern-like, shade

Alchemilla alpina – dark green, divided leaves, silver beneath

Alchemilla mollis – light green, rounded, hairy, sun or semi-shade

Anaphalis triplinervis – grey leaves, good habit, sun

Anthemis cupaniana – low mats of silvery feathery foliage, sun

Artemisia – various silver and grey, sunny positions, poor soil

Arum italicum pictum – spearhead shaped, deep green marbled white, sun or shade

Asperula odorata – spreading, bright green, whorled, partial shade

Astilbe – fern-like leaves, often coloured, moist position, semi-shade

Baptisia australis – glaucous green, bushy, full sun, 3 ft

Bergenia – bold cabbage-like, semi-evergreen, sun or shade

Cynara cardunculus – elegant, deeply cut, silvery grey, sun, 5 ft

Dianthus – silvery grey, spreading

Dicentra – delicate, finely cut, glaucous greens, sun, semi-shade, 1 to 2 ft

Dictamnus albus – leaves like an ash-tree, gleaming, good habit, sun, 2 ft

Epimedium – various species and hybrids, delicate foliage, semi-shade, 1 ft

Eryngium – various species, handsome silvery-green, holly-like foliage, sun

Euphorbia epithymoides – light green and bright yellow, spring, sun, 1 ft

Euphorbia pilosa major – yellow bracts in spring, bronze autumn tints, $1\frac{1}{2}$ ft

Euphorbia sikkimensis – bright red, young shoots, yellow bracts, sun, 4 ft

Foeniculum vulgare (Fennel) – feathery foliage, sun, 6 ft

Geranium macrorrhizum – dense, light green, rounded leaves, shade, 1 ft

Geranium renardii – sage-green, lobed, sun, 9 in.

Geranium sanguineum – heavily cut leaves, low spreading, 1 ft

Gunnera manicata – enormous bold leaves, boggy conditions, 6 ft

Helleborus corsicus – large spiny glaucous evergreen leaves, partial shade, 2 ft

Helleborus foetidus – dark evergreen green, deeply lobed leaves, sun or shade, 18 in.

Hemerocallis – long, arching, bright green, sun or partial shade, 2 to 3 ft

Heuchera – attractive, spreading habit, leaves like a Virginia creeper, 1 ft

Hosta – wide variety of sizes and colours, very handsome, moist soil, sun or shade

Iberis sempervirens – dense, low spreading, dark evergreen leaves, 9 in.

Iris – various, spikey leaves, very decorative

Lamium galeobdolon variegatum – attractive, well marked with silver, shade, 1 ft

Libertia formosa – narrow, iris-like, evergreen foliage, sun, 1½ ft

Mentha rotundifolia variegata – light green mottled silvery white, 2 ft

Morina longifolia – rosettes of spiny leaves, decorative, 3 ft

Nepeta faassenii – grey-green aromatic foliage, sun, 1½ ft

Origanum vulgare aureum – spreading mats of dense small leaves, yellow, sun, 9 in.

Paeonies – all have handsome foliage

Polygonatum multiflorum – arched stems with bold dark green leaves, semi-shade, 3 ft

Pulmonaria saccharata – green tongue-shaped leaves, marbled white, shade, 9 in.

Rheum 'Bowles' Crimson' – very large bold foliage, damp position, 8 ft

Rheum palmatum – leaves large, rounded and strikingly lobed, damp position, 6 ft

Rodgersia – handsome bold pinnate or palmate leaves, heavy textured, peaty moist soil, sun or shade, 3 to 4 ft

Ruta graveolens (Rue) – evergreen, glaucous compound foliage with tiny leaves, sun or half-shade, 1½ ft

Saxifraga umbrosa (London Pride) – rosettes of evergreen leaves, dense mats, 9 in.

Scrophularia nodosa variegata – green leaves striped with cream, sun, 2 ft

Sedum maximum atropurpureum – deep maroon, fleshy leaves and stems, sun, 2 ft

Sedum spectabile – dense clumps of celadon-green leaves, 1 ft

Stachys lanata (Lamb's Tongue) woolly grey leaves forming spreading mats, with 18-in. flower spikes, sun

Thalictrum – various, dainty glaucous foliage, 3 to 5 ft

Tiarella cordifolia – spreading masses of heart-shaped leaves, shade, 9 in.

Tiarella wherryi – leaves similar, less rampant, shade, 9 in.

Veratrum nigrum – bright green, large pleated leaves, borne on upright stem, sun, moist soil, 3 to 4 ft

Verbascum bombyciferum (*broussa*) – great spreading rosettes of silvery grey woolly leaves, followed by woolly grey spikes to 10 ft, full sun

Index

220